June 27, 2003

Gary

I hope U
this book as m
as I have.

A publication of the Flyfishers Club of Oregon
and its Flyfishers Foundation

McKenzie River Edition

Cover photo by Dan Callaghan: Member angler, below the Goodpasture Bridge, one of the last covered bridges in Oregon.

CONTENTS

Distributed by Frank Amato Publications
Printed in Thailand
ISBN 1-57188-275-8

ACKNOWLEDGMENTS

This journal's cover would not have been graced with Roderick Haig-Brown's classic and cogent comment had not his neighbor, Van Egan, casually mentioned to us the McKenzie connection. It has become our gem quote from among Haig-Brown resources located in University of British Columbia archives for us by young Arn Keeling, with approval of Roddy's daughter, Valerie Haig-Brown. How fortunate!

Similarly, the on-target comments of esteemed Barry Lopez (Page 147), would have escaped us, and our readers, had it not been for the interest of Joan DeCamera, of Vancouver, WA, daughter of icon guide Merl "Mac" McMullin. Her interest? The impressive river photo, filling two pages of Life Magazine's July 1987 edition featuring Lopez's essay was taken directly in front of the McMullin's McKenzie home. (Joan also filled in what might have been blank spaces in her father's signal story, as did the family's attorney, friend and fishing companion, Robert D. Lowrey of Eugene and Dr. Timothy J. Campbell of Portland, a longtime client and friend of Mac's as well as member of this club.)

Another most fortuitous circumstance was to find the Rev. Peter Webster boyhood chum of Richard Brautigan, popular hippie generation author living just a few miles north of the editor's fjord home and oyster patch. The anecdotes Reverend Webster provided, before semi-retirement locally and his moving away to another pastorate, added fresh, piquant flavor to that story; the oysters he took in return were equally fresh but contained no such "pearls."

And who could provide better authenticity of Mackenzie/McKenzie origins than Canadian university history professor and author, Barry Gough of Ontario, an authority on the very subject!?! Beyond his book, First Across the Continent/Sir Alexander Mackenzie, Professor Gough has the background to share additional insights ... and does. The result is both interesting and enlightening.

Rich details of Herbert Hoover's Oregon boyhood were provided by the great grandson of his boyhood chum. Robert Graham Landrum of San Antonio, TX, let us utilize the private, unpublished memoirs of Elmer E. Washburn, a favorite companion of young Hoover. A rare candid photo of Mr. Hoover on the McKenzie was furnished by the daughter of his personal pilot, "Hard Hat" Johnston — Mrs. Sharon Johnston Erlenkotter, Santa Monica, CA. Other photos appearing here are publicity pictures taken by the media or from official Hoover archives.

It isn't enough for old newspaper accounts and other forms of the written word to flesh out a personality as gentle yet forceful as that of the late Chris Jensen, arguably an Oregon fish biologist worthy of high ranking among the west's best-ever. The reader will get some special insights into Biologist Jensen, thanks to his son, Chris, Jr., who remains an Oregonian, and Chris' younger sister, Jan, now an Idahoan. (And thanks, as well, to Tom McAllister for his early outdoor articles and column comments; Tom saw that Jensen's programs were assuring better McKenzie fishing when many others weren't so sure.)

We stick our editorial neck out, perhaps, by selecting one McKenzie guide's wife, Tuck Thomas, to convey our thanks to all the other guides and their wives, and all the anglers and their wives who made input into the unique substance of this journal. Tuck opened more doors and tracked down answers to more questions than any of the other contributors, as many and as cooperative as there were. A so-called "complete" listing would still remain incomplete, as it does here.

Finally, some recognition to the club and foundation officers who ignored the few naysayers in setting a new publications course by authorizing the Rivers of Oregon series.

Leadership's ground-breaking actions were inspired, to no little degree, by a double handful of unsolicited checks – ranging from $25 to $1,000 -- from enthusiasts for the River Series concept. Those enthusiasts were Donald H. Bates, Jr., Miami, FL; Stephen D. and Elizabeth Bechtel, Jr. (Foundation), San Francisco; C. Morton Bishop, Portland; John M. Davis, Sparks, NV; Joan DeCamera, Vancouver, WA; John C. Hampton, Portland; Mike E. Henningsen, Portland; Alec Jackson, Kenmore, WA; Randy Labbe, Portland; Robert D. Lowry, Eugene, OR; Dixie Monkhouse, San Rafael, CA; Rowland K. Rebele, Aptos, CA; Bill Rosenfeld, Portland; Garrett P. Scales, Rosa, CA; Roger Schaad, Beaverton, OR; Willis Schaupp, San Francisco.

The Creel, traditionally a 32-page journal of eclectic topics, now continues in book form of flyfishing histories of some the state's most favored rivers, beginning with the McKenzie; similar histories of the Umpqua, Rogue and Deschutes already are in various stages of production.

The Creel Commitee

Mark Metzdorff, MD, Chairman Ex Officio
Lenox Dick, MD, Chairman Emeritus
Bob Wethern, Editor
Roger Bachman, Production Executive
Greg Smith, Art Director
Doug Lynch, Art Director Emeritus
Dan Callaghan, Chief Photographer
Tom McAllister, Historian
Frank Amato, Marketing Manager
Cal Cole, Foundation Representative

FOREWORD

McKENZIE RIVER—BEGINNINGS

Earliest records verify that McKenzie River fish were important to locals and visitors alike. Their abundance was as impressive as their variety. The 90-mile waterway, flowing westward from Cascade Mountain resources, was home to native "redside" rainbow, cutthroat, and bull trout. Hatchery rainbow and steelhead were introduced much later.

But it was the toothsome spring Chinook salmon which annually brought Warm Springs Indians west through McKenzie Pass, and Klamath Indians northward on game trails for many, many moons. Early white settlers noted but did not date their first sightings of Warm Springs tribal folks' long journeys from eastern Oregon—at first on horseback only and later in horse-drawn wagons—to catch and then take their dried fish home as winter provisions.

"I have reason to believe that these same Indians or their ancestors had been coming to this place (just above present Leaburg damsite) long before any white men were in the area because in a flat, each time it was plowed, arrow heads and flint came to the surface."—Clem Carter, second generation McKenzie Salmon Hatchery official in 1978.

"The Indians, who utilized every part of the salmon except intestines, made soup out of the heads," Carter continued. "They took only what they had room to properly care for in their camp (where Hendricks Bridge State Campgrounds exists) Squaws did most of the work with the fish while the men took care of the livestock."

Still later, when salmon hatchery egg-taking operations drastically reduced the Indians' annual harvest potential, they were given the gutted carcasses of female fish.

"You did not have to worry about anything being taken by them, as they would not take anything unless given to them," Carter explained.

So it was in the late eighteen hundreds. The celebrity naturalist and fishing guide, Prince Helfrich (1908-1971) relayed McKenzie status reports from still earlier old-timers:

".... a clear, cold river untouched by man and teeming with trout and salmon .... so abundant the largest trout would average 14 inches .. . because there was not enough food to produce large fish."

Helfrich again:

".... the old-timers tell of driving out of Eugene, with their wagons and teams, and fishing the lower river for two or three days, or until they had a wagon load of fish to take back into town to sell. As the fish population diminished, larger rainbow up to six pounds were common. Then, with additional fishing pressure, the great numbers of fish started to decline so that in the early 1940s the fish population was in an alarming state."

More than fishing pressure had the river on a slippery slope.

"Our records show two to three sprayings of DDT post WWII into the early 1960's. Intent was to spray for epidemic populations of spruce budworm that were defoliating trees in the upper positions of the watershed... almost 1,000,000 acres."—John Allen, District Ranger, McKenzie District.

The resultant massive insect and fish kill energized further a seminal wildlife field agent already focused on nurturing declining fish populations back to health—Chris C. Jensen (1916-1987). Central to his five-year plan was a 14-inch trout limit to protect dwindling numbers of spawners. That was not nearly as popular as some of his inventions and techniques vastly improving trout trapping and planting programs. A partial benefit of Biologist Jensen's vision and energy, in his own words:

"Results so far prove that we raise fish in hatcheries until they are legal size or over, the trout show up in greatest numbers in the creels. We estimate that 28 per cent of fish in that class provide some angler the catch he is after."

What follows, by Robert Leo Heilman in his Real Life in Timber Country, speaks of the Umpqua River, to the south. But the application is universal, especially for the McKenzie:

"The river's pace is not a human one. Our longest personal measurement, our own life span, is barely enough to begin measuring the rate of change in a river. And, of course, even that requires careful attention, decades of accurate observation."

Heilman continues:

"It takes a long time to understand a place, to learn what its limits are. The beaver were trapped out between 1820 and 1841 and with them went the thousands of small dams they built. Hydraulic gold mining silted up hundreds of miles of gravel spawning beds. Moving logs downstream scoured the bottom. Marshes were drained to make pastures. Cattle and sheep grazed the streamside brush, causing erosion as the banks gave out. Clear-cutting removed thousands of acres of forest canopy. Following the flood of 1964, the federal government began a program aimed at removing woody debris from the headwaters creeks, turning them into what might as well be concrete storm drains."

The full story of man's triumphs and failures along the McKenzie River will never be completed. Hopefully, with more guardians in the mold of Prince Helfrich, Chris Jensen, and others about to be profiled, the McKenzie River's future holds more ups than downs. Indeed, if past is prologue, this eclectic collection of angling experiences may give clues to the future of a famous Oregon stream that naturalist and outdoor writer Tom McAllister has called:

".... the mother river for driftboat guiding in the Pacific Northwest."

—The Editors

Chapter 1

Upfront

Dan Callaghan photo

Al Severeid photo

RODERICK HAIG-BROWN

Roderick Haig-Brown's name and fame are known universally among fly-fisherman. Almost virtually unknown is that he picked Oregon's McKenzie as a study model for his early book, Return To The River, the life cycle of a spring Chinook salmon.

In the process, he came to respect the McKenzie's trout bounty, as indicated in his own heretofore unpublished words on this journal's front cover. Haig-Brown's on-site research seems to have occurred as the Thirties became the Forties. That fact would've remained unknown had it not been for ongoing conversations between Haig-Brown and his near neighbor on the Campbell River. Van Gorman Egan, himself an author of contemporary angling books, was an early fan of Haig-Brown's classics. Visits from his Wisconsin base to Vancouver Island, and to Haig-Brown's Above Tide home on the Campbell, eventually led to Roddy's encouraging Van Egan to become a neighbor and fishing companion.

Though their time frames on the McKenzie weren't the same, that Oregon water often was the grist of their conversations, which included Roddy's wife, Ann, who had accompanied him there. Van Egan felt there must be some physical evidence verifying Roddy's time on the McKenzie. Initial, informal research revealed nothing.

But four hours by a professional archivist, Oregonian Arn Keeling, in special collections at University of British Columbia, produced the sought after hard evidence you see here. Daughter Valerie Haig-Brown, herself well known in the world of angling literature, encouraged and aided in the research, and gave permission to use this material.

A common thread in the "McKenzie connection" was that both Haig-Brown and Van Egan were impressed with the dry flies dressed by Stella S. Ely at the shop she and her husband, Smith Ely, established in the Thirties at Blue River. Elsewhere, we chronicle the widespread admiration for the durability of Stella Ely's high-riding patterns. Van Egan:

"I believe there are still two or three patterns tied by the Elys in the Haig-Brown collection." Return to the River was just the fifth of 27 books which Haig-Brown had published during his lifetime. Daughter Valerie has extended the Haig-Brown books by another five titles. Initially, for Return, Roddy used a working title of Spring, The life Story of a Columbia River Chinook Salmon. Haig-Brown:

Dan Callaghan photo

"... but the publishers don't altogether like that." Later he explained that an "inspired editor" at Morrow, George Labaire, chose the ultimate title from one of the manuscript's several sections. The name "Spring," which Roddy had given to Return's main Chinook salmon character, remained intact, and the McKenzie remained her natal river.

Did Roderick Haig-Brown ever actually fish Oregon's McKenzie? His longtime neighbor and fishing companion isn't sure. What Van Egan is sure of, he himself did not wet a line. He was too busy scratching out a living for himself and his young bride, Maxine. Van Egan left his lab job at a Canadian pulp and paper mill when a 1957 strike closed the plant. Maxine's sister proposed they come to Oregon. Frances Engelbrecht had built up a solid bar/restaurant/trailer park business in Blue River called Forest Grove. The good times were accelerating as preliminary construction activity was begun for Cougar Dam on the McKenzie's South Fork.

"Maxine's sister got me a job with a logging company clearing land at the proposed impoundment site," Van Egan remembers, "but I wasn't much of a logger and lasted only a couple of weeks."

During the winter months of '57-'58, he tended bar at Frances' Forest Grove, which was prospering greatly as a result of heavy patronizing by loggers and rock drillers building the dam.

"There was a particularly interesting hard rock explosive man known as 'Blackie,'" Van Egan remembers. "I made up a wild and woolly drink that I named the 'Rock Driller Killer,' and Blackie ordered it regularly. It was a real 'booster,' and had a pretty fancy price for those times — something like seven or eight bucks!"

The closest Van Egan got to McKenzie fishing during those mid-winter months was to visit the old Ely fly shop in Blue River.

By then, Smith Ely was gone and Stella continued her role as the shop's main force. Van Egan muses:

"Most of the Ely flies, particularly those tied for the McKenzie, were made of deer hair bodies and hair wings — high floaters for the fast waters of that river. I rather think with the Elys gone, so are their distinctive fly patterns. "Too bad!"

Neither Van Egan nor Maxine fished during their 1957-58 McKenzie stay, but she had on earlier visits to sister Frances' Forest Grove enterprise.

"They fished for trout in a slough just off the main river, and later floated with one of the famous McKenzie river guides who eventually lost his life in a drift boat accident," Van Egan recalls. "I think he worked out of Thomson's, but was not a Thomson. Frances had worked at Thomson's lodge earlier. In fact, when she cooked at Thomson's, her homemade wild berry jams were favorites of Herbert Hoover when he stayed there."

EPILOGUE—The Van Egans returned to British Columbia and their Campbell River home, having successfully end-run the long mill strike, and resumed their neighborliness with the Haig-Browns. Sister Frances retired to Waldport, Oregon, where Alzheimer's claimed her in the fall of 1998. Her once-thriving business no longer exists in Blue River. Van Egan's first book was Tyee, history of the famed Campbell River salmon competition, followed more recently by Waterside Reflections and Rivers on My Mind.

THE McKENZIE QUESTION

"THE MACKENZIES WERE THE MOST NUMEROUS OF ALL HIGHLAND CLANS, AND THE NAME POPS UP ALL OVER THE PLACE (WITH VARIOUS SPELLINGS)."

—(Barry Gough, *Professor of History*, Wilfrid Laurier University, Waterloo, Ontario, Canada)

So explains Prof. Gough, author of First Across the Continent/Sir Alexander Mackenzie, to the question of how Canada's Mackenzie River was named for Sir Alexander (1762-1820) while Oregon's McKenzie honors a younger cousin, Donald Mackenzie (1783-1851).

"They were distant cousins—that's as close as I can come," the historian advises. "Sir Alexander was born on the Isle of Lewis, Donald near Inverness. I am at a loss to show the direct link."

Indeed, they were distant—and different—in many ways, including appearance. The king's painter-in-ordinary, Sir Thomas Lawrence, reveals a startling personality of Sir Alexander. There is in Mackenzie's countenance, as captured by the court painter, the burning glow or appearance of knowing. Windburned cheeks hint at his years of frontier toil. A dimple in the chin gives a youthful impression. Reddish blonde hair, unruly and shaggy, frames a broad forehead, immense eyebrows, and remarkably dancing eyes—eyes that show at once intelligence and the look of undoubted success.

That success was assured when, by age of 31, Mackenzie had become the first white man to cross North America from the northwestern hub of the interior trade, Lake Athabasca, in present-day northern Alberta, to the Pacific Ocean. He had opened the continent to trade and exploration. Inscription on an imposing rock still bears onsite testimony to his river discovery "Alexander Mackenzie, from Canada, by land, 22 July 1793."

Sir Alexander, a man of enormous ego and overpowering ambitions, returned to his homeland late in life to be knighted, marry and lead a more genteel life, leaving behind a Metis family in North America. (Abridged from Prof. Gough's biography of Sir Alexander.)

Donald Mackenzie left Scotland for Canada in 1801. By 1810 he was a veteran Indian trader when John Jacob Astor recruited him as a partner in the fledgling Pacific Fur Company, headquartered in Astoria, OR. Shortly he was chief factor.

Donald's skills as a marksman and woodsman—plus his huge, corpulent body, his weight estimated at 312 pounds—assured his leadership role. Out of earshot (no doubt), he was called "Fat Mackenzie," but was admired for his absolute fearlessness and extraordinary energy. His habit of being on the move constantly when not asleep led to a contemporary offering another nickname, "Perpetual Motion."

So it was in April of 1812 that Donald Mackenzie led a party of six from Fort Astoria up the Willamette River valley to a major tributary they named "Mackenzie's Fork."

By late June they had returned to Fort Astoria. Mackenzie, considering record-keeping a drudgery, brought back only brief traveling notes in personal hieroglyphics on beaver pelts. Apparently he reported the area not worth Pacific Fur's attention, and turned to explorations elsewhere.

How did the Mackenzie Fork become the McKenzie River? Historians offer no clues, other than to say that both spellings were used interchangeably through the years, until common usage gave McKenzie the nod.

There was one aberrant spelling that did not survive. In 1869, a river crossing was dubbed "McKenzie Bridge," and a post office opened there in 1874 also bore that name. Locals protested for years until, in 1918, the name was changed to McKenzie. Long before the name change, the first postmaster, Philander C. Renfrew (1817-1880) shot himself, becoming the river valley's first reported suicide.

—The Editors

LAMPMAN'S McKENZIE

Oregon's fauna, flora and fish so stirred the creative juices of Ben Hur Lampman, a Midwestern flatlander, that for twenty years until his death in 1954 he was the official, uncontested Poet Laureate of this state. Some of us Lampman readers still accord him that honor.

This club's twelfth president, the late Herbert Lundy, longtime editor of The Oregonian's editorial page, in 1973 once summed up Lampman's 35 years of all-around talents lavished on the daily. Lundy wrote that they "... established him not only as a literary master, but as an authentic, sensitive naturalist and humanist."

Lundy recalled that "Ben was once a great fly-fisherman, but reverted to more contemplative angling in later years." That may explain Lampman's The Coming of the Pond Fishes, Binford & Mort, Portland, 1946. In it he assumes a reportorial stance in placing smallmouth bass in the McKenzie/Willamette system, as follows:

"Peter Pierson, Eugene, says he first caught smallmouth bass between Harrisburg and Peoria about 1930. John Hall, Eugene, says he caught them first near Eugene seven or eight years ago. Bill Lupher, Eugene, now dead, caught smallmouths in 1933.

"Ray Matteson, of a Eugene sporting goods store, says that L.D. Collier, Springfield fly-tyer, and Obak Wallace, Springfield, have caught smallmouth bass near the Ferry Street Bridge at Eugene for several years. Mr. Matteson declares he has confirmed the identity by counting the rows of scales on the cheeks.

"John Hall and Peter Pierson say the smallmouths are found as far up the Willamette as Cottage Grove; that they are caught in riffles and are splendid fighters. The wet fly is used.

"The anglers report that the Willamette smallmouths characteristically are found in fast water in the fall, but in spring are found at about the spot where you would retrieve your fly if you were fishing for trout."

Lampman's sources and Ben himself aren't now able to answer our questions—How often did a smallmouth angler, fishing with a wet fly, hook a trout instead? And, would it have been considered an incidental catch?

FRANK WIRE: A RIVER IMPRINT

BY TOM MCALLISTER

No man enjoyed the bounty of outdoor Oregon more than Francis B (Frank) Wire (1879-1966). Few men knew so vividly the impact of growth and change.

It began in 1890 on a virgin and unfettered McKenzie River when a 10-year-old was imprinted while fly-fishing with his dad, Melville C. Wire, a Methodist minister.

The zest for fishing and then hunting never faltered until, at age 87, Frank joined in death his fellow Spanish-American War volunteers of the 2nd Oregon Regiment. Many died from an unseen enemy in the Philippine campaign, malaria and dysentery. Frank said he was shipped home to die but recovered pronto on returning to his McKenzie haunts.

Photo Courtesy of Oregon Journal

Wire building his five-spline rod.

That long ago war year of 1898 was also noted by Frank as the only season he didn't get a buck. When he was 86, Frank's doctor said "no" to another buck hunt on Steens Mountain.

But that following May of 1966 Frank returned to Glimpse Lake, Canada, for Kamloops trout on the sedge hatch with patterns he tied for this annual outing, Carey and Nation's Specials and Black O'Lindsay.

Enroute to Canada that spring, Frank stopped to address the Inland Empire Fly-Fishing Club in Spokane, WA. Fenton Roskelley, outdoor writer for the Spokesman-Review, took the man he called "a legend among Oregon hunters and fishermen," to cast from a small tippy boat on Badger Lake.

Frank outfished Roskelley, himself a durable angling legend, and fellow outdoor writer, Rex Gerlach. Frank belted 60 to 80-foot casts hour after hour without a sign of tiring. His weary hosts tactfully told Frank as the day waned that they were getting a wee tired.

Through two chill and windy days he regaled his hosts with stories of fishing past and market hunting deer, pheasant, duck, snipe and grouse to put himself through the University of Oregon.

He took them 75 years back when McKenzie River "redsides" were visible everywhere beneath surface slicks where tall Douglas fir, alder and dogwood extended a wall of shade. They admired Frank's stout fly rods. Frank used skills he acquired as an apprentice cabinet maker to create a five-strip bamboo rod.

When they came ashore for a lunch rest, Frank quaffed his glass of milk, downed a sandwich, strode onto the dock and resumed casting. For him, eating was a waste of good fishing time. Frank never took stimulant, never used a swear word in his life and was a consummate gentleman.

Never without red silk neckerchief.

"And he's tough as an old hickory board," commented Gerlach who marveled at the stamina of the 87-year-old on what was his final grand outing.

In his outdoor column following their first and last encounter, Roskelley wrote, "We doubt we'll ever again have the privilege of fishing with a remarkable fly fisherman the likes of Frank Wire!"

In 1889, when Frank's dad first took his two sons by horse and buggy to fish the lower McKenzie near Hayden Bridge, the watershed and fishery was intact, as much so as when Donald McKenzie led a party of exploration to the river in 1812. The Pacific Fur Company men could've fished a long cane pole with a braided horse hair line and a spinner or strip of fillet from a whitefish, but the Reverend Wire expected his sons to fish with a fly only. This classical man, who taught Greek and Hebrew at Willamette University, first brought his family to Eugene from Illinois in 1884. His ministry as a circuit rider carried past many a reach of trout water, those boys at his heel.

Frank said his father didn't tie his own flies. In fact, almost no one did in those days because fly patterns sold commercially for a dollar a dozen. They always had a short gut attached; the loop on the gut was looped into the leader. Patterns were limited and mostly feather wound, except for the few hackle flies. Some of the old McKenzie standbys for the Wires were

Royal Coachman, Professor, Grizzly King, Gray Hackle, Brown Hackle, Blue Bottle, Rueben Wood and White Miller.

Large hooks were in vogue. Frank said his father carried No. 6 and hardly ever any flies smaller than No. 8. That said something about the size then of those native McKenzie trout. From Frank's personal memoirs:

"These flies had gut attached, and father bought silk worm gut and made his own leaders. He didn't have a bamboo rod, but used lancewood. I remember that he was always breaking and splicing it. Then, he got bamboo poles and made guides of wire. They were strong but hard to handle.

"He always was a conservator and when we had enough fish to eat he stopped us. There were lots of fish in those days and it was hard, sometimes, to make us stop fishing."

Considering the abundance of rainbow, cutthroat and bull trout competing for space and food, it's small wonder McKenzie anglers often took 75 trout a day, after a limit was set at the turn of the century.

The Wires fished from the bank. Guided drift boats were yet to evolve. Early transport for freighting or log drives was with fir planked and tarred skiffs, sturdily built to withstand boulder pounding.

At Hayden Bridge, young Frank got his first lesson in respect for and care of one's catch. His father saw Frank's creel held uncleaned trout already gone soft and pallid. He told the boy to either take his licking or give up his fishing privilege for the rest of the trip. Frank took the licking.

Reverend Wire set the pattern and gave his sons the freedom to adventure into the wilds of the upper McKenzie country, summer after summer.

They soon knew it from origin in the chill spring fountain at Clear Lake to Willamette River confluence.

Market hunting was a natural outlet for the brothers. At age 15 Frank was in the business with his brother, Melvin.

"We had a choice of plowing for 50 cents a day, from dawn to dusk, or shooting pheasants at four-bits a pair," Frank told the writer in one of many visits in his home where he taught fly tying to my oldest son, Scott, and more who came to the source. Frank was a natural teacher and shared his fly tying and rod building skills in the basement of his Portland home. He wanted his rod-building style carried on, as he said, "after I've kicked off." Eventually his rod form, tools and bamboo supply were passed on to one of his "boys." Frank used that term for young or adult alike. A serious fan of Frank, also a longtime Oregon fly club member, Dean Jones, continues to repair Wire originals and to make his own rods in Wire's style.

To keep his bird dogs from getting footsore, especially when pursuing what he called "Denny Pheasants" in the grain stubble of the Willamette Valley, Frank had a string of four dogs, Llewellyns and English pointers that he alternated in pairs. Judge Owen Denny, US consul general in Shanghai, first introduced the ring-necked pheasant into this country. The initial release was on his farm near Lebanon. Pheasant numbers exploded in the habitat perfection provided by the diversified farming that prevails throughout the Willamette Valley.

Cereal crops, hay meadows, untilled fence corners and undrained cattail and steeple bush swales provided ample food, nest and escape cover. It was Frank's early object lesson in wildlife management. Now, the valley is nearer a biological desert for pheasants and meadowlarks but hosts of Canada geese now choose to winter in the clean open expanse of grass seed, clover and winter wheat.

Frank's market outlet was Portland where he shipped by rail most of his game to a Mason & Company. On his best day he bagged 85 pheasants in the swales along Soap Creek in Benton County. The Wire brothers began shooting with single shot 20-gauge shotguns until their dad let them use double guns. They hand-loaded and reloaded their brass shells in the field. Frank remembered:

"The wads worked loose and we always had shot rolling around in our pockets."

When they duck hunted, the Wappato beds were so thick they carried a scythe to cut a surface opening for their decoys.

Frank chuckled often over the memory of the market operator who guaranteed, in writing, 50 cents for all the big ducks and 35 cents for all the small ones they could provide. When Frank delivered 50 big mallards, the man recanted but paid $75 for both the ducks and the letter of guarantee.

The Wire brothers packed horses up the McKenzie and followed the deer trails through the Cascade crest where both blacktail and mule deer summered. When they began market hunting deer they realized $10 each for the hide and a sack of jerky.

To preserve their venison they used a drying rack. They carried spool wire which they strung between stakes, cut the venison into strips, sprinkled on coarse black pepper to ward off flies and used sun, wind and smoke of alders to cure their product. It was brought to market in muslin flour sacks.

The teenagers often camped near game trails above McKenzie Bridge. They called this "Big Prairie." The brooding heights of Lookout Pass set well back from the river. There was a natural meadow for grazing their stock, and wild strawberry and huckleberry bushes abounded in the adjoining burns. They sometimes camped alongside Indians from Warm Springs who followed an ancient pathway over McKenzie Pass. Many Indians continued down river to pick hops on valley farms.

Others stayed behind to spear or gig spring Chinook. The salmon arrived in June and waited on a long summer in deep, dark upriver pools for the onset of fall and spawning.

Occasionally, the boys camped in abandoned mine, homestead or timber claim cabins built with materials at hand—pole frame, split cedar siding and peeled cedar bark for roofing.

They pulled slabs of bark from moldering ancient firs and leaned them against poles for a quick bark shanty shelter.

Sometimes they joined sheepmen in their camps in the high country under the Three Sisters and Mount Washington. That first season, Frank said they climbed the South Sister at a gallop and were both "... tougher than tight knots."

September, when the blacktail moved to the lower country, was their best time for prime animals. The Wire boys picked up game trails easily visible in the light volcanic ash and followed down country to a stream crossing. Here, they made a blind and waited from first daylight until noon.

Frank used a single-shot 45-70 Sharps rifle and kept one shell in the palm of his left hand for a fast reload.

His lankly liver-and-white setter, Aguinaldo, was there to trail any crippled animal. Frank named Aguinaldo (Ag for short) for the daring young Philippine revolutionary who fought both Spanish and Americans to liberate his country. Ag was also Frank's best-ever bird dog. He said they had an understanding between them that only comes a few times in a lifetime of owning and working dogs. Ag took his work in stride and was never headstrong or rattle-brained. Frank's constant companion would smell the deer and look at Frank as much to say, "here comes one!"

Netting a B.C. Kamloops trout.

Frank would let the deer come to within 50 yards at the crossing and take a neck shot.

On one unforgettable shot a four-point dropped in its tracks. Frank leaned his gun against a log and walked over to bleed the deer. Ag was trained to stay until called.

The buck jumped up and Frank said, "It's eyes were green and I knew I was in for it." Before he could call the dog he was wrestling the buck by the horns. When he yelled, Ag was there to grab the deer by the throat. The buck struck with its front hooves. Ag would let go momentarily but grab again until Frank got his rifle and an open shot. His lesson was never approach any large game without keeping gun in hand.

The stories about Ag in the old McKenzie hunting days rolled out as we sat at Frank's fly bench. Frank would carry out a deer "shot pouch" fashion by interlocking the legs. One evening when Frank was packing a deer to camp, Ag growled, barked and leaped ahead on the trail and into a spitting, snarling melee with a cougar.

Bill Vandevert, rancher near Farewell Bend (present Bend) on the Deschutes invited the Wire boys over to hunt and fish. They crossed from the Willamette Valley up the McKenzie and over the Scott Trail in five days with six packed mules. Rancher Vandevert turned out to be the real beneficiary. The boys took 20 hefty rainbow on flies right in front of the ranch to give ranch hands a change in diet. More, Frank shot a bear and rendered it for lard.

Deer were scarce, but after horseback hunts of a week's time they left a spike, a fork and a three-point for the ranch table. Frank remembered that three of their Deschutes rainbow totaled 15 pounds.

After completing university studies, Frank again was on the move, this time as a traveling furniture representative. His fly rods were at hand, and he always arranged business in Medford to coincide with the best of the Rogue summer steelheading.

He was appointed director of the old Oregon Game Commission in 1932. Before his long tenure, directors came so fast the employees couldn't keep track, and fish stocking was one form of political patronage.

Frank was also the man who oversaw the transition of this peanut-sized state agency—directed largely by local whim and political appointees— into a professional fisheries and wildlife agency, now the Oregon Fish & Wildlife Department.

His toughest challenge was the population explosion of mule deer—and the crash on the Murderer's Creek range in Grant County. It was akin to the Kaibab episode in Arizona. The doe was held sacred as part of a long effort to rebuild herd numbers. Cougar were nearly liquidated under the old $50 bounty. Nature, in her own harsh way, corrected the situation through starvation. Deer died by the thousands on winter ranges stripped of browse. Deer stood on their hind legs to prune the juniper trees, a last resort diet.

The public howled when Frank supported his newly minted wildlife biologists who said the herd had to be drastically reduced—this on top of the winter die-off—if there was to be any range recovery and future for the deer.

Sportsmen's groups and receptive politicians were out to get Frank and his boys with their fancy ideas right out of Oregon State University. Frank, the man from an earlier era, had an overview of fish and wildlife history and ushered in modern game management in Oregon by hiring those first graduates ... then backing them!

He was called to the office of then Governor Charles H. Martin and asked "to put the lid on." Frank stood his ground. Martin, a former Army general, as Frank told it, said:

"You go manage your game and I'll handle the (invectives) politicians."

After 15 years, Frank resigned following a heart attack, but returned as secretary to the Oregon Game Commission where he was like a director emeritus for six more years. Included in his sage input was his observation that market hunting did, indeed, speed the coming of game protection measures, but that no amount of protection can bring back wildlife once the habitat is destroyed.

Frank brought about the first-ever "fly fishing only" water in the region, Davis Lake in the upper Deschutes country.

And, he had a direct hand in banning angling from boats in the heart of the Deschutes Canyon.

Importantly here, it should be reported that Frank had a personal concern about the unraveling of the McKenzie fishery. He got his commission to set in motion a five-year study of catch returns from wild versus hatchery trout and the survival and true costs of artificial plants. Long fyke nets were used in the Leaburg Canal to determine the strength and timing of downstream migrant salmon and trout and their losses in power diversions.

Chris Jensen, the first fishery biologist assigned to the McKenzie under Wire's watch, wrote in the third year of that study that while the spawning areas were intact the cover sufficient and natural food plentiful, the potential brood fish were being removed from the stream by anglers before they reached maturity. Jensen wrote:

"The anglers can do their part by being satisfied with a catch of immature fish and by returning to the stream large fish that are ready to spawn."

That set Wire in motion. He backed Jensen's proposal for a 14-inch maximum length limit to protect the native McKenzie rainbow. The 14-inch rule prevailed in spite of an at first incredulous audience of fishermen.

But, Wire and Jensen had stature and the McKenzie River Guides Association joined in support of the beginning of a new era in trout stream management—not just on the McKenzie but, slowly, across the land.

Frank was neither a joiner or a man who worked to garner titles and honors. His whole being centered on sharing the virtues of being afield with rod and gun and treating it as a privilege.

There are three personal items of Frank's that the writer remembers as a part of his attire and times:

One was the stout hickory wading staff that Tom O'Neil in Ashland made for him in 1915 when they rode out in the evenings to seek steelhead on the Rogue's riffles.

The second was the 1879 gold piece on his watch chain. That was his birth date and his lucky charm. Finally, he was never without a red silk neckerchief on his many hunting and fishing outings.

Frank Wire was part of that golden outdoor era that we can only dream about. He transitioned into the present and helped us see how much we lost and why we can never stop trying to regain Beulah Land.

CHAPTER 2

GUIDES AND THEIR WIVES

Sister John photo

From left: Dixie Monkhouse, Guide Wade Thomas, Jaques Coveny, Janet Conrad.

The guide's Wife

By Marjorie L. Helfrich

Many articles have been written about guides—Indian guides, Alaskan guides, and whitewater guides. But of the guide's wife, very little has been said. And yet the wives of the guides here in the Northwest play a very important part and are quite as essential as the rest of the guide's equipment.

Here on the McKenzie, a successful guide must be able to run a boat, know fishing water, teach the dude to cast a fly, and entertain his passengers when fishing is dull.

But his wife also must have diverse capabilities. Her main job, of course, is to prepare a tasty lunch and drive the car for the fishing party. It is also handy if she can back her own boat trailer, entertain the fisherman's wife, and send along an apple pie for the midtrip cookout. She must be able to answer the questions almost all fishing parties ask. From experience, the wife knows beforehand what the fisherman and his wife will want to know. Almost invariably, after introductions, it goes something like this:

"How many children do you have?"

"Do you fish too?"

"Do you stay up here all winter?"

"How much snow do you have?"

"What do you do all winter?"

After these preliminaries are over, everyone gets down to the real business of the day—where to fish and what flies to use. The fisherman's equipment must be checked and, perhaps, a line greased.

Finally the party takes off with the guide's wife going along to bring back the car and trailer. The boat is launched, tackle set up, and an hour of take-out agreed upon. By this time it is almost noon, and she is free to go back home and begin her day's work.

The guide's wife takes care of all business calls and correspondence and hires guides for the extra trips that come along. In her spare time she must manage her home and raise the children, make jam and take care of the garden. It goes without saying that an appetizing dinner must sometimes be served as late as 9:30 in the summer when best fishing is late.

Often she is asked to loan the facilities of her refrigerator or deep-freeze so that the fisherman's catch may reach home in fresh condition.

Occasionally she may have to make an extra trip down river to pick up the fisherman's wife, who has become bored and wants to go home early.

After a long day on the river the guide is tired. His day has been spent with a fisherman who has made "birds' nests" with his line, hooked a bush on every backcast, and flicked the nervous guide's ear with his fly. He is in no mood to be trifled with, and the wise wife does not pick this time to bring up unpleasant subjects!

Instead, she is tactful and a sympathetic listener, getting her husband in the mood for another day of fishing tomorrow!

Marjorie Goodpasture easily recalls practical examples of what Marjorie Helfrich was addressing, as follows:

"When Bob, my husband, was guiding seriously, I used to drive for him. Before that, when we were much younger, I fished with him many times, often catching two at a time when using a dropper fly. More recently, when my son Jim was guiding, he'd have his fishermen leave their car at the takeout, so they could take him back to his rig. Don't think he ever had a driver.

"Waiting for your man to come off the river, especially after a big thunder and lightning storm seems forever. And there are scary 'near misses!' Up at Eagle Rock, where it appears you'll smash into it, one of a pair of Bob's clients got so scared he jumped out of the boat and onto that rock! Rowing back upriver was impossible. Rope lines had to be rigged to pull Bob's boat back up for the rescue."

Bob Goodpasture's early guiding now and then involved humor, as his wife relates:

"Bob used to get those guys who, y'know, took the trip more to drink than fish. He always laughed recalling the dude who thought he was flyfishing in great style, but his fly was hardly more than arm's length from his rod tip!"

Robert F. "Bob" Goodpasture took over the family filbert farm but guided until the mid-Forties, when his expertise at cabinet making attracted Sears Roebuck and other major outlets. He died at his home in mid-November of 1996.

Helfrich Dynasty

DY-NASTY—A RACE OR SUCCESSION OF KINGS, OF THE SAME LINE OF FAMILY; THE CONTINUED LORDSHIP OF A RACE OF RULERS.

—*Webster's New International Dictionary, Second Edition, 1934*

Few knew the reasons why Ben and Ruth Helfrich named their first-born "Prince." Many more eventually became aware that it signaled the beginning of an astonishing American out-of-doors dynasty.

In just sixty-three years, Prince Helfrich (1907-1971) achieved respect of world leaders and kings of commerce for his multiple role-modeling—as an environmentalist, a molder of youth, and river guide pioneering far beyond his McKenzie River home base. He died too soon, of cancer, shortly after exploring drift boating possibilities of yet another difficult and untamed British Columbia river.

From Tom McAllister Files

"He always wanted to try a new river ... to see what was around the bend,"—(Dave Helfrich, *senior son of Prince and Marjorie Helfrich*)

These days, the Helfrich dynasty of river guiding expertise extends beyond Dave and his brothers, Dick and Dean, into the third generation. All guide for a living and belong to the McKenzie Guides Association, as fellows—Dave's son, Ken; Dick's son Jeff; and Dean's sons, Adam, A.J., and Aaron.

In some respects, Ben Helfrich set the course the clan has followed to this day. Ben and Ruth Helfrich, with young Prince in tow, left Prineville country to operate, with Uncle Jim Helfrich, a big ranch out of McArthur, CA, southeast of Mt.Shasta, but sold it just before World War I. Prince's folks moved to the McKenzie in 1912, later lamenting the fact the war boom likely made the California property more valuable. They bought, for $5,000, a mile of McKenzie riverfront, timberlands and large meadows totaling 160 acres. They built a large home and general store eventually named "Halfway House" as it became an overnight midway stop for horsemen traveling through McKenzie Pass to Eastern Oregon

"I remember as a child, my grandmother working in the store. She sold food, fishing tackle and pumped Union gasoline with one of the old gravity type pumps."—(Dave Helfrich)

Dave's mother, Marjorie, recalled in her memoirs:

"Later on, Ben Helfrich built cabins on the riverbank, and the guests he took on fishing trips were the beginning of the Helfrich family fishing and guiding business."

How did Prince come by his given name? During those first twentieth century years in Prineville, Ben and Ruth developed a warm friendship with a forest service employee named Prince Glaze. A generation later, Dean Helfrich was named for the investment celebrity, Dean Witter, a client and close family friend.

❧❧❧

Gradually, the country became less wild and less sparsely settled. Even so, ill-tempered dogs often heralded Warm Springs Indians' annual arrival to trap and net salmon and pick huckleberries. When not fighting local dogs, they often trotted beneath their owners' wagons, out of the sun's hot, fall rays. Soon air near Hendrick's Park reeked with smoky stench of drying and decaying fish.

"The Indians camped under the apple trees and the annual trading and exchange of news began. Homesteaders traded deer skins and other pelts for moccasins and gloves. The skins were picked up one fall and the finished products were delivered the next."—(Marjorie Helfrich)

Prince and Marjorie were sweethearts as students at the University of Oregon. Graduating a year ahead of him, she taught a year at Mosier on the Columbia River. Prince majored in geology, but his heart was one with Marjorie. And, it turned out, outdoorsy things other than geology. They visited her Klamath Falls home and were married that year, 1931. But the McKenzie Valley beckoned.

Circumstances were primitive when Prince first began guiding in the early Twenties. He started on the mile of waterfront his grandfather owned above Nimrod. Guests at Ben Helfrich's Halfway House and cabins were rowed out in the river by Prince to fish. It was a quiet stretch, before major floods washed away Clover Point, rapidly increasing the gradient.

In those early days, considerable physical exertion was required. Prince bridged the long interval between heavy and crude boats of planks, up to 18 feet long and only three feet wide in the middle, and the modern McKenzie drift boat. Often it took four men to load the former on flatbed wagons, not today's light, rubber-tired trailers.

Then, a horse team would haul the boat upriver for the next day's fishing. Eager anglers, following behind the horse drawn rig, savored the imminent experience.

A four- or five-mile downstream run was enough to all but load the boat with fish—and river water. It was necessary to carry a big water bucket for bailing after running certain rapids (Clover Point, Martin, McAllister, and Gate Creek) which often filled the boat to the floor boards.

"... if a guide came in at the end of the day not soaking wet to the waist, he had not put in much of a day!"—(Prince Helfrich in Tales of the Oregon Cascades)

Sometimes dubbed "old scow," early boats still provided fly fishers opportunity to fish pocket water.

Between guiding seasons, young Prince did some trapping, until World War II, when pelt values dropped and logging became an essential wartime occupation. As his guiding business grew, he traded loggers boots for buckskin, his signature guiding attire.

Prince guided out of Thomson's Lodge, then the McKenzie facility most favored by visiting anglers. By 1947 he launched his boys' camps project at the insistence and support of a Portland doctor, Leon T. Goldsmith, who was impressed with Prince's close ties to Mother Nature.

"Goldsmith encouraged me to take a groups of youngsters up in the high country and teach them how to fish, how to camp, everything connected with the outdoors. The first year he rustled six boys for me to make it sort of pay. From then — Prince had been in this business for 14 years when he made these remarks — the numbers jumped to eleven boys. then fifteen, and now this past year I handled 67 boys."—(Prince Helfrich, before the Flyfishers Club of Oregon)

By then, Prince had five different camps for boys, ranging in ages from eleven to sixteen, among them Skyline Boys Camp. The younger boys were taught the basics ... tent erection ... fire building ... camp cookery ... gunfire ... horse handling and, of course, fly casting.

"We (had) a program for those thirteen and older, including a trip down the McKenzie in boats where the boys get to handle their own boat quite a bit of the time. For boys who liked horses, we (had) a horseback trip of ten days. Then, we did backpacking trips, carrying all our needs for a week into a wilderness area. That was the toughest on me of anybody! Trying to keep up with those boys, while carrying a heavier pack! —(Prince Helfrich)

Helfrich reminded flyclub members of a pleasant bonus:

"A lot of you fathers should know how rewarding it is to participate in these experiences. I get to see your son when he catches his first fish! Often, upon hooking his fish, he'll start running backwards, maybe fall over a log, jerk the fish out of the lake and fall on him. Invariably, the BIG fish would get away!"

Which led to a regular evening campfire routine. Every night, in turn, the boys got a chance to tell their comrades of the big one that got away!

"And, while their stories were largely actual and factual, they were launching a tradition for future campfire exaggerations!"—(Prince Helfrich)

Boys camps and McKenzie River guiding didn't make for year-round income. Prince and his crews also were pioneers, opening so many western whitewater rivers for others to follow.

The Rogue and John Day remain regulars in Helfrich offerings. Olympic Peninsula streams provided fall and winter steelhead floats for Dave, Dick and Dean. Prince didn't guide on peninsula rivers.

A first ... one-time only trip ... recalled by a Metolius River summer cabin lessor, gives hint that pioneer river running was not all fun and games:

"With another seasoned guide, Veltie Pruitt, Prince made a 1938 run of the lower Metolius which some believed would end in disaster. A San Francisco financier, John Gallios, and his wife, had acquired old Heising Ranch and meadow for their summer home, and Gallios wanted to run the river in that area.

"Gallios and a Marine officer friend, 'Captain Jack,' were in good hands, fortunately. Because that drift, amongst great ponderosa pine logs locked in bank to bank in some places, necessitated twenty portages! When they put in at Canyon Creek, many said they would not come out of that canyon. But, three days later, they arrived at the old Mecca Bridge at Warm Springs on the Deschutes River. The Gallois summer home later became Eleanor Bechen's House on the Metolius Resort."—(Tom McAllister, McKenzie Creel historian)

❧❧❧

Another unusual float that Prince remembered was the largest his crew ever launched—on the Middle Fork of the Salmon River:

"These ten fellows, almost all Texans, wanted plenty of baggage boats to be sure there was room for their five cases of whiskey. We had five baggage boats, including the whiskey boat! There was plenty of whiskey for the ten dudes and the fifteen guides!

"Next season, friends of those Texans had only two cases. The whiskey boatman was a beginner and tipped over in one of the Salmon's bad places. Barron Hilton was in my boat at the time and, not paying too much attention to the water soaked guide, we went after the whiskey. A case of Old Quaker, in a nice pine box, hit a rock and completely disintegrated and the bottles sank out of sight, just as we were about to retrieve them.

"So, we took out after the case of Old Grandad, and caught up with it. Barron reached out and lifted it off the top of a big wave, and got it in the boat—just as the paper carton gave way! But, we saved Old Grandad!"—(Prince)

Logistics were a great deal simpler on the home river in earlier days when horse-drawn rigs were replaced by automobiles/trailers for transport of fishing parties. For years thereafter, wives of guides, or other family members, were pressed into service as "drivers." Guides knew where to launch and take-out for half-day or full-day trips. Accordingly, drivers were dispatched to take-outs with autos and boat trailers to await arrival of the guided parties.

"During my days as a driver, I often had the children along. More recently, guides hire drivers."—(Marjorie Helfrich)

❧❧❧

Traditions originated during fishing days on the river. The midday break in some comfortable glade for a fresh trout lunch was a welcome trip highlight. Prince used a 21-inch diameter frying pan.

"We'd throw a whole pound of butter in and get the pan hot while skinning those last-caught trout. That was just like taking a glove off your hand, eliminating any fishy taste. Then, rolled in flour, they were salted and pan fried!"—(Prince)

Another tradition still practiced by guides today is having the inexperienced fly-fisherfolk refloat their dropper fly. The technique almost always assures that even novices will hook up to a fish, and is one reason for the McKenzie's universal popularity.

"If my fisherman can really handle a dry fly, then he'll single fly. With dudes who can only get out 15 or 20 feet of fly-line, a dropper fly is added and refloated to the surface by raising the rod tip. That dropper fly technique probably originated right here on the McKenzie!"—(Prince)

As senior spokesman currently for the Helfrich clan, Dave adds extra dimensions centered in the family business.

His apprenticeship with his father began at age twelve by being the driver backup for the boat takeouts and camptending. Shortly, however, he was running a drift boat on the upper river.

"My first customer on the McKenzie, in 1945, was Lee Johnson, early member of your Oregon flyclub. My day book records I only made $4.50 that year. And I only had four trips! The next year I made $62.50 and was well on my way to my first million!"—(Dave)

The Helfrich name was perpetuated in other venues. Prince was a charter member and first president of the Oregon State Guides & Packers Assn. He also was a charter member of the McKenzie River Guides Assn., and vice president at the time of his death.

Some sidelines in the late Forties were tree farming and a bit of trapping locally.

Senior members of the Helfrich clan often developed more than casual guide/client relationships and, as a result, enjoyed special perks.. Allen L. Chickering of Woodside, CA, retired senior member of a prestige law firm, was a member of the famous Greenhead Club in the Sutter Basin.

"Dad and I used to shoot ducks at Greenhead, its clubhouse stilted to escape high runoff from the Sacramento River. We shot there for five years, courtesy of Allen."—(Dave)

Chickering married Marshal Fisher's widow and for nearly the next quarter century they enjoyed the summer home and a fishing lodge called "Bright Waters," upstream from McKenzie Bridge. "Fisher was well-connected, and during the rationing days of World War II he kept Dad's rolling stock in hard-to-come-by tires."—Dave)

Other prominent captains of industry, political leaders and celebrities valued Helfrich friendships. The late Walter A. Haas, Jr., honorary chairman of the board of Levi Strauss & Co., who had been guided by three generations of Helfriches before his death in 1996, was highly complimentary of his relationship with the family:

"Prince taught me most of what I know about fishing and instilled in me a love of the simplicity and beauty of outdoor life. He was way ahead of his time as an environmentalist and conservationist, recognized nationally by being asked to testify before Congress on related matters years ago.

"He saw the great possibility of Zane Grey's property on the Rogue River. I would never have considered acquiring and developing it without his encouragement and counsel. It has been a great joy to me and my family for 25 years."—(W. A. Haas)

Former governor of Oregon, Robert W. Straub, had believed Oregon's rivers were just rivers—until he and his wife, Pat, had floated most of the wild ones with Prince.

"Running rivers with Prince made them come alive! Camping out with Prince, I noticed birds would come closer to his campfire with their songs, and deer were more visible and calm. Nature knew a kindred soul in Prince."—(Gov. R. W. Straub)

Dave Helfrich verifies that his father fished some with Herbert Hoover when Hoover stayed at Holiday Farm:

"But, mainly the President fished with Fred Harris."

Tributes to Prince Helfrich, who set the standards for his clan and others to follow, are impressive, collectively. An individual standout, however, was penned by Edward E. Merges, who was a law student in the Twenties when invited to Sparks Ranch by his father and an associate. Folks at Sparks recommended Prince as a guide and so began a friendship expressed in Merges' touching words:

"Probably the most unusual thing about Prince was his personality and ability to help others appreciate the outdoors. Our campfire nights ... Prince's harmonica mingling with the sounds of night ... are vivid in my memory.

"I like to think there will always be another time when I return to camp, perhaps chilled and certainly hungry, and Prince will pull out a piece of beef jerky for an appetizer while he prepares campfire biscuits in an iron pot."

TRAPPER MAC

MERL "MAC" McMULLIN
1905-1999

Development of McKenzie River country could have taken another path, had Merl "Mac" McMullin been one of the six in Donald Mackenzie's exploration party. Their brief visit in 1808 to assess fur trade potential resulted in Factor Mackenzie's negative report to his Fort Astoria partners. A concentrated fur harvest in the McKenzie watershed and beyond still was many decades away.

By skills and by inclination, McMullin—as great a drift boat guide as he became in his own time—always favored trapping over river-running. It wasn't just because the money often was better, but rather his apprehension since voiced by his daughter, Joan DeCamara of Vancouver, WA:

"Dad once told me he was more comfortable trapping than guiding. He worried he'd have a stroke or some disabling circumstance that would put his fishing clients adrift without his expertise."

That concern almost became reality in September of 1996. Dr. Timothy J. Campbell, who champions McMullin as the McKenzie's best-ever guide, explains:

"Dad (Dr. Charles Campbell) and I were back at Mac's house this particular fall morning to finish back-to-back dates. Mac came out, said he wasn't feeling too well ... had a funny sensation in his left eye. Dad, who was an internist, recognized right away he was having a precursor to a stroke. With Daughter Joan's help we got him to a Eugene hospital where he completed the stroke in the middle of the night."

McMullin survived then, but that ended a fishing client friendship with the Campbell's begun right after World War II. The doctors, fittingly, were Mac's last clients. His last river drift, as a passenger, was with his son, Randy, just a year after his stroke. Mac's account of that final trip as remembered by Daughter Joan:

"Dad was too busy advising his guest how to fish the McKenzie, and pointing out local historical points of interest, and giving Randy a tongue-in-cheek bad time about his drift boat techniques, to do any real fishing himself. But his impaired left arm didn't stop him from catching a couple of fish."

Highlight in his final days of confinement was the McKenzie River Guides Association personally presenting Mac with a plaque attesting his seventy years of river guiding. He checked out during the McKenzie's March Brown hatch, May 23, 1996.

How it all began is a remarkable saga worth detailing here. Mac's father, Seth Albion McMullin, was a small rancher/farmer in the Springfield area and, as Mac remembered, "did a lot of hunting and fishing." From high school, McMullin enrolled at Willamette University on an athletic scholarship, intending to eventually become a coach. After three years, however, funding was tough and Mac decided he liked nature's quiet places better than people anyway. He went to work for the U.S. Forest Service, including fighting forest fires.

The Campbell/McMullin relationship had already begun. They were roommates in the Sigma Tau fraternity—the senior Campbell the pre-med student and McMullin the football player hoping to become a coach.

Dr. Tim Campbell learned from his father that they used to borrow one another's clothes for campus social events.

Their special lifelong relationship was rekindled when Dr. Campbell returned from World War II and resumed his western Oregon fly-fishing, this time with Mac, who in 1947 had begun guiding actively on the McKenzie.

It was a learning process. And in that learning process Mac guessed he wore out twelve or fourteen drift boats. In a 1992 taping he explained:

"I never had a serious accident, or totaled one out. It was just the wear and tear on 'em ... the bottoms would go bad, even though you painted 'em up and took care of 'em as best you could."

Mac, who evolved into a masterful boatman and superb fly-fisherman, was not adverse to reveal early mistakes. Mac again:

"The first boat I ever had ... I was kinda new to the game ... and decided I'd have a real fancy-looking boat. The whole thing was mahogany veneer! I varnished that thing up so it'd shine! It didn't occur to me at the time that, boy, if it looked so nice to me, what were the fish going to think!?! It didn't take long to camouflage that one, and all the rest have been painted a kind of green color."

Tim Campbell remembers his introduction to McMullin on the McKenzie right after World War II when he was eight or nine years old:

"I remember sleeping under the line deck. As a kid I was small enough to curl up there and sleep while my Dad fished.

"The usual routine, when I was a boy, was we'd leave Portland early, driving down old Hwy 99 West, and up McKenzie Highway, arriving at Mac's around 10 a.m. Mac usually called it a day about dark. On the way home we'd either stop at Dairy Queen in Springfield or have dinner in Eugene."

In those early days, young Campbell had been relegated for several years to the wet fly or worm or salmon egg. That changed abruptly in the early Fifties when a fine hatch had his father busy catching and releasing trout on a dry fly while Tim went fishless on a wet pattern.

"Finally, I said to Dad, "gimme that thing!" He gave his rod to me, with a few rudimentary lessons on what to do. Of course, I'd watched him for years! I started dry fly fishing on that very spot. Don't think I drifted a wet fly ever again, except for planters when we were short of fish for the midday fry."

There were other Portland anglers who developed father-son traditions with Mac and supporting guides. At one time the season's annual opener involved Dr. Len Dick and son, Spencer; Ed Francis and son, Win; Charlie Miller and son, Eddie; Spencer Erhman and son, Spencer, Jr.

But as memorable as those associations were, none had the deep, enduring relationship with McMullin as did the Doctors Campbell. From boyhood, Dr. Tim developed an admiration described in superlatives:

"Dad was a superb fly-fisherman, but Mac was the best I ever saw, and I've seen a lot of 'em (referring to icons of the Golden Gate Casting Club in San Francisco). The reason I know is, he let us do what no other clients could -- row while he fished. He first let Dad and then me row so he could fish! He was an absolutely fantastic fly-fisherman, just unbelievable the way he could cast."

Dr. Tim describes their relationship as " ... kind of like family," explaining:

"We had an awfully good time. Early on, Dad would row so Mac and I could fish. When Dad got more infirm and was unable to cast very well or for much time, Mac would let me row and he would fish, just a wonderful fly-fisherman!"

The traditional noon fish fry was a favorite of the Campbells and easier to supply in a time when both native and planter trout could be kept. Dr. Tim:

"Mac had the same old frying pan, wonderfully seasoned, for as long as I can remember. He never believed in getting one of those long-handled jobs so popular on the river, always favoring his short-handled one."

McMullin, it seemed, had endless energy whether afloat or ashore on the family's twelve acres there on the river. Timber for the family home came from old growth fir on a hill behind.

Nearly half a mile up that ridge, Mac piped clear creek water to the house. A mule hauled the pipe, which had to be buried manually. Because he loved fresh vegetables, he tended an impressive garden each season.

Dr. Tim was impressed that while Mac was " ... a tireless worker..." he moved so deliberately it never looked like he was doing anything. Dr. Tim:

"Whether cutting the family's firewood or mowing the big lawn or anything like that, Mac always looked like he was just lollygaging along. Then suddenly, when you looked up, the job was all done! He was just amazing that way!"

One season, Mac put in 43 straight days of river guiding. He knew the "right" way to do all things, and he was Missouri mule stubborn about anyone trying to help him, even when he was 90 years old. It was a matter of pride to him. Dr. Tim:

"Hell! I'd known Mac for fifty years, but he would not let me help crank his boat onto the trailer. He did it exactly the same way every time to get the boat seated and tied down, the way he had been doing it for seventy years! He was as amazing when working as when guiding."

Bob Wethern photo

Of his guiding, McMullin had characteristics and routines unique to himself. One was he never used an anchor to maintain a steady holding position in the river. Daughter Joan:

"He did it the hard way—he rowed! From years of rowing he developed the most massive fingers and hands."

Mac's preference and ability for strong rowing created many special upstream dry fly opportunities for the Campbells which other guides seldom, if ever, gave their clients, according to Doctor Tim:

"Mac loved to fish upstream. Guides not in the same league with Mac, and a few other hardy old-timers, usually have you fishing down river the whole trip. When apparently about to pass up a likely stretch of water, Mac — with a hard pull against the current—would move in just downstream. Then, he'd reverse his boat and we'd enjoy dry-flying in less pressured water."

Partly because of his encyclopedic knowledge of the McKenzie's most productive waters and the ability to many times make the water work for him, McMullin was never in a race with other drift boaters to get afloat first. Dr. Tim:

"He never wanted to be the first. So, he'd sit around at the landing with his party, tying flies on leader tippets and just diddling around until all the more anxious boatmen had taken off."

According to Doctor Tim, Mac could put his clients into fish behind those lead boats, so they were never handicapped. Even age and dimming eyesight didn't substantially handicap McMullin. Dr. Tim:

"Amazingly, Mac never ever wore glasses! The light bulbs over his fly tying desk at home got brighter and brighter ... more and more wattage ... as the years passed.

"And, during the last 15 years of his guiding I noticed he'd always stop in sunshine to tie on a new fly. Never, ever wore regular or dark glasses. When I'd tease him and offer him mine, he'd counter aw, glasses ruin your eyes!"

His eyesight was good enough to save a teenage girl from a watery death. Mac recalled his clients, a San Francisco doctor, fishing with his wife, had just caught a trout on the river's south bank, above Blue River. McMullin:

"We landed it and, like any boatman, I glanced upstream and down before returning to the current. Directly across from us I thought I saw the head and shoulders of someone clinging to a river rock. My clients agreed, so I started pulling across. About midstream, my clients started yelling to a fellow in a rocking chair on the north bank who apparently was reading and hadn't noticed the crisis just a few feet beyond him. As he ran to the shore, the girl let loose and the fellow waded in and grabbed her. My doctor client gave her first-aid and an ambulance from Blue River took over."

One of Mac's "rescue" roles was more humorous than serious. A rubber raft carrying five or six had upended in Browns Rock currents.

They got to a shallow tailout, where one of them asked McMullin if he would bring their raft downstream and ashore. McMullin:

"I was doin' a pretty husky job of rowin' but couldn't make headway. Finally realized that the seat backs of the upside down raft were catching the current, like a sea anchor!"

Another insight into Mac's Good Samaritan character is related by Randy McMullin's wife, Janet:

"Our family was overnighting with Mac and had all gone to bed when Mac roused Randy about ten o'clock because he'd heard someone on the river yelling for help. They launched a boat for a night rescue despite the pitch black darkness. The rest of us drove down the road and, with help of a state patrolman's flashlight, located a man huddled on a large rock. Wet, cold, and frightened, he first refused to board the boat as it paused momentarily in the current, thanks to Mac's rowing ability. When Mac had to row upriver again, Randy convinced the man it was either in the boat next try or on the rock all night! The man got in!"

Witnessed by Grandsons Rick and Tim, they considered Grandpa the greatest river guide ever, and their dad pretty brave himself for just going along to help. Then, as often, McMullin shunned the limelight, but had a competitive streak, according to Dr. Tim:

"Mac and the better-known Prince Helfrich had a professional rivalry, though basically they were good friends. Reserved Mac would quietly try to outfish Prince and other icon guides. And, from my recollections, usually did!"

McMullin guided a lot of celebrities ... Clark Gable several times ... and had the president of Standard Oil of California, H.C. Mattie, in his drift boat when a group of President Hoover's friends were on the McKenzie. McMullin:

"I never did boat with Hoover personally. And, I wasn't one of the many guides who claimed they had, once Hoover passed on. Hoover liked to boat with Fred Harris. How they met was a stroke of luck for Fred."

Harris was an off-season caretaker for Buck Travis, president of Greyhound stage line, who had a summer home near McKenzie Bridge, according to McMullin. Harris guided during fishing seasons. Hoover's friendship with Travis led to his meeting Harris. McMullin's further memories of that illustrious angling pair:

"Hoover did mostly sit down fly-fishing. Smoked a pipe as often as circumstances allowed. Harris was kind of robust ... a well-framed fellow ... a very good boatman who did a lot of guiding out of Thomson's Lodge, one of the oldest if not the first lodge on the river."

Interesting fish tales seldom have impressive collaboration, but one that struck Mac's funny bone was verified by no less than the late Thomas H. Tongue, former justice of the Oregon Supreme Court. In his privately printed Confessions of a Fly-Fishing Judge, Tongue relates how in 1980 he hosted an English friend on several Oregon rivers, including two days on the McKenzie:

"... days of excellent fishing with Mac. Somehow, and several times, my friend hung his back-cast fly on limbs of trees along the river. Finally, Mac very gently asked how, with such back-cast problems, he got along in England. The reply was,'where I fish in England the banks are mowed!"

"Mac has never forgotten that! Later, my son visited my English friend in London and was taken to fish in one of his favorite rivers, and its banks were, indeed, mowed!"

"Once I knew what to expect," McMullin later reported, "I kept my English client away from shore!"

Justice Tongue's verdict on Mac:

"Mr. McKenzie! Without a doubt the best guide on the McKenzie and is "booked solid" during the fishing season. His "little fingers" are thicker than my thumbs!"

Mac would never tell Tom his age, but Tongue figured if Mac had played fullback for Willamette University in the late Twenties, he had to be well into his eighties during their association extending to 1992. He marveled:

"... rowing a McKenzie drift boat nearly every day of the trout fishing season, then running a trapline in the winters in nearby mountains (and more distant waterways)—pretty strenuous for a man in his eighties!"

An adult lifetime of trapping, plus other physical chores, had McMullin in outstanding shape, with woods wise sense that would've made the fur trappers of yesteryear very envious. Dr. Tim:

"Mac often told us that trapping was his first love, and that he would retire from guiding before he'd quit trapping. Dad and I went with him several times on short traplines. Those of his routines he didn't actually show us, he described in exciting detail."

Including one winter when he nearly died. Mac had a full pack and traps and was snow-shoeing across thin ice, disguised by snow, when the ice broke and he fell through. Somehow he survived, in a solitude where the only help was his own. The Campbells didn't go on those week long trap runs, but Dr. Tim felt as though he had been along:

"Mac always had a good car, one that would take him aways up in the snow. He'd take off for a week, clear to the base of the Sisters mountains ... hell and gone up there, all by himself! Must've had food caches along the way (in metal bear-proof garbage cans) he would stock up in early fall. He was skilled enough to live off the land with jerky and little else."

Among the routines that Mac shared with the Campbells was trapping the McKenzie from his boat. He found fish-killer otter in log jams and harvested them to a point just short of extinction. Dr. Tim:

"He could tell by looking when drifting down river where the beaver had come in and out of the McKenzie. He was pretty careful, never trying to clean them all out and do away with his opportunities the next season."

Mac opted for shorter handled fry pan than McKenzie tradition.

McKenzie neighbors were grateful for his trapping skills. Vivienne Wright, former owner of the famous Holiday Farm, had Mac solve a flooding problem caused by beaver between the farm and the river. And a North Bank Road resident used to get Mac to trap out troublesome beaver on his property.

He trapped far beyond the McKenzie and Willamette watersheds, as far as Oregon's Malhuer Refuge and California's Tule Lake Refuge. Just as Mac was becoming a journeyman trapper he got, so the story goes, a crash course in outdoorsmanship. Bob Lowry of Eugene, longtime friend and client and sometime legal counsel to Mac recalls:

"There was a rugged individual named Harry Hayes, who, since 'the teens,' had considered the Three Sisters country, including Separation Creek, his private trapping and hunting preserve. That was often, when he wasn't at the Mckenzie Bridge Store operated mostly by his wife. Harry and Mac got crossways for awhile on Sisters area rights when McMullin first showed up there, but Mac somehow sweet-talked Harry into showing him the deer herd routes that the cougar followed and special trapping techniques and places—everything!"

Hayes' lessons paid off, and just about everything was fair game. McMullin:

"Yeah, mink, muskrat, otter, beaver, coyote and lynx or bobcats ... quite an assortment."

Dr. Tim adds:

"When he was younger, in the Forties and Fifties, Mac had hounds to track down mountain lions. The cougar bounty then was $60, which was a helluva lot of money! In later years he'd trap bobcats for their pelts. And, by some arrangement with biologist friends at Oregon State University, he'd furnish bobcat skulls for their studies."

McMullin not only trapped for himself, but also for the federal government, on the refuges many times with Ennis Nestle and Earl Jeans, who later became guides. Of those days, Mac said:

"I don't like to be bragging about it, but one season I caught 6,200 muskrat! Trapped 4,000 on the Klamath and Malheur refuges alone. And I was just one of maybe nine other trappers around Malheur Lake!

"Sounds excessive to some, I guess, but in fact, those rats should've been thinned out a little more. The very next summer was dry, the lake's shoreline receded, throwing all remaining muskrats into smaller areas, where they became diseased and died off. I don't think there were any muskrats there to speak of for 15 or 18 years after that. That's Nature's way of taking care of over population."

Just as he did with any personal project, McMullin practiced perfection in his care of pelts. Dr. Tim:

"He did his furs himself. Home from trapping, he'd go into his basement and skin the animals himself and set up his own furs. I can remember watching him nail down a beaver pelt."

As a result, Mac always got top dollar for his pelts at fur trappers' shows and came home with many awards for excellence in fur handling. Dr. Tim:

"He took really good care of them. Fur shows at Canby, as far as I know, put Mac as close to Portland as he ever got. He'd go down to Eugene for a haircut, but Dad had a hard time prevailing to set him up with an internist there. He just didn't like the cities!"

Mac was a real McKenzie man in all respects! He knew the watershed as intimately as the waters within: Dr. Tim:

"Mac had a lot of respect for the water. I don't think Mac ever ran Martin Rapids, at all, in the last 15 years of his guiding career. He may have taken a client through there, just so the client could say so. But he didn't care much for that water."

As a result, Mac never lost a client, but he did dunk a client once, according to Dr. Tim:

"He had a big, tall guy—about six-foot-eight—standing in his boat when it hit a rock. The tall fisherman sort of lost his balance and flipped out!"

Guiding and trapping consumed most of Mac's time, holidays included, and there was little left for personal leisure. He once said that being around fishing enthusiasts so much sort of compensated for those times he couldn't scratch his own fishing itch. Dr. Tim agreed:

"Mac didn't do much in the way of a vacation. He'd go over to the beach, particularly when he was married to Mary ... take a few days off and go crabbing on the coast."

Early planked boats were cumbersome and testimony to guides' river boating skills.

—For non fly-fishing clients, Mac had a special boat rod made by his friend, Earl Jeans. It was a 5 1/2 fiberglass rod with old Medalist reel and a "killer" fly something like the Spruce Fly pattern. The combination accounted for many McKenzie steelheads, including one by Friend Lowry.

Mac's effectiveness resulted, in part, from his day's end routine of clearing the catch, examining stomach contents and then sitting down at his fly-tying desk to create representations before retiring that night. Lowry:

"I was never much of a fisherman but knew I was with the greatest guide, thanks to Judge Tongue's strong recommendation when I was a petitions clerk for the Oregon Supreme Court in the Eighties."

Lowry describes his best action with Mac:

"A big swirl indicated a bull trout strike so Mac advised I let out line.

After a scrappy fight, the line slackened momentarily, then picked up again. Ultimately, we pulled in a planter rainbow on the terminal fly that was as limp as a rag, having been squeezed almost flat by the big bull trout before it gave up. On the dropper was a 17-inch redside, Mac thought attracted to the fly by the commotion caused by the bull trout."

Lowry recalls that the biggest redside Mac said was ever caught in his boat measured over twenty-three inches and was taken from "The Rock Garden," just upstream from Mac's home.

The Doctors Campbell also were among the very few who actually witnessed Mac's own fishing interests and skills, and developed such a strong bond that, even today, Dr. Tim is saddened when relating how it ended:

"Dad was never the same after Mac had his stroke. Dad had prostate cancer and realized they would never, ever fish together again. Seems he decided it was no longer worth it. Even so, I arranged with a good young guide, Don Morgan, who reminded me of a young McMullin, to take us out.

"It was an absolutely gorgeous spring day in May. Dad didn't fish much but caught a couple for our noon fish fry. At our lunch spot, Dad laid down for a nap on grassy sand while Don and I hurried up a little firewood. Dad had said he'd just as soon die on the McKenzie as any place he could think of, which worried both of us.

"But, he woke up and we had our fish fry and went on about our way. That was the last time Dad was on the river and, obviously, a bittersweet memory for me. For many years, though, we had a helluva good time together on the McKenzie with our friend, Mac!"

LEROY'S MARK AND BRAND

Beyond his father's icon shadow, Leroy Pruitt easily and early established his own mark and brand on McKenzie Valley and elsewhere. Though steeped in family drift boat traditions, he pioneered sweep boat river running of the McKenzie and other Oregon rivers. And, the horses remaining on the Pruitt ranch of Shelly and Leroy, still bear Pruitt's unique brand—a wedding of the capital letters "L" and "P."

Dan Callaghan photo

Leroy was introduced to a "sweep" or pontoon boat being utilized by Don Smith on the Salmon River's Middle Fork when the Smiths were hauling supplies for the Pruitt's downriver floats. Leroy sized up the clumsy 33-foot craft, once a military bridge pontoon, exclaiming:

"That's when I said, by golly, I'll get me one!"

He located one in a huge military surplus store in Las Vegas. The challenge of downsizing for more maneuverability tested Pruitt and Dick Helfrich, who helped him shorten the boat to 25 feet.

The rayon fabric reinforced neoprene pontoon was cut in half. Six feet of mid sections were removed before the remaining ends were painstakingly sleeved together, with a two-foot overlap to assure a waterproof seal. The two-foot overlap was sealed with a special contact cement. But not without problems. Leroy:

"We had glue up to our armpits, but I had the first pontoon boat on the McKenzie!"

Pruitt put his innovative craft to good use through the Sixties and Seventies—running day trips on the McKenzie in between longer floats on the Salmon's Middle Fork and eastern Oregon's Owyhee. The McKenzie one-day trips were scenic floats with a popular cookout. Leroy:

"I'd stop and make Dutch oven biscuits and fried chicken and have a nice salad and lots of coffee. That was our lunch! All for $10 a person!

Outfitters still make good use of sweep boats. The Helfriches still have several and Steve Schaefers has one. For years Leroy helped his Dad with other family enterprises, running camps for teens and hunting parties in the Steens Mountains. Pruitt:

"Once I started my own river business, that kept me away from the mountains a good share of the time. Still, I did book a couple of adult and family trips to the Steens during the month of August, between Salmon River runs in July and Rogue River runs in September."

The Pruitt family name remains prominent among outdoorsmen. Leroy's first cousin, Bob, was a river guide and outfitter. Leroy:

"We made many trips together, a mix of the Salmon's Middle Fork, the Rogue and the Owyhee."

His mother, Ina Pruitt, was a fine artist, close companion to her family, and a helping hand when her frail circumstance allowed. She tied and sold dozens and dozens of flies, supplying local guides and a national market as well. Leroy:

"As a kid, I would watch her at the fly vise. I learned from her, naturally, and mostly have tied my own flies since. Fly dressings have always fascinated me. I have some tied by the Elys and a box, also, of flies tied in the east which President Hoover sent to my Dad."

For Mrs. Pruitt's contributions, the family, in turn, always tended to her "roughing it" needs. Leroy:

"She had a special, gentle-saddle horse, and her art supplies were always carefully packed. There also was a special tent for her and Dad, with a good, comfortable bed, little throw rugs, and all that."

What especially delighted Mrs. Pruitt at that high camp was the daily routine of feeding the numerous deer. Leroy:

"They would come out of the quaking aspen woods, mostly at evening time, near our cabins and corrals. Mother would have 10 or 15 deer eating out of her hands. She got such a thrill out of that!

DON WOUDA

Football scholarships have long helped assure quality McKenzie guides. The late, great Mac McMullin may not have been the first. He certainly was not to be the last. Nor, likely, will Don Wouda of Springfield, recruited to Oregon from Colorado in 1958.

Wouda grew up fishing his summer days on the Platte River. Once an Oregon college athlete, he focused on the McKenzie's South Fork. Wouda:

"I'd get off (part-time) work, drive up there to fish—until dark—a couple times a week. Ted Bryant taught me how to tie flies... and how to use them. He was with me on my first McKenzie guided trip in 1966. Did my first Rogue trip with Prince Helfrich the next year, and the Salmon's Middle Fork in '73. If I'm any good it's because of the technical experience I learned there."

Dan Callaghan photo

Wouda and his wife, Jennifer, met skiing at Mount Bachelor in 1969. Although not a fly fisher she, according to Don, likes to state that she brought her own hip boots into the marriage. His guiding years, including 27 with Dave Helfrich and most recently with Steve Schaefers, have framed his views on guide/wife relationships:

"Years ago, we guides had a saying that there were two kinds— 'divorced' or about to be divorced. 'A more current quip would be, 'Show me a fulltime guide and I'll show you someone who either is single or his wife works fulltime.' "

Jennifer Wouda fits that later category very nicely. An active career as an Elementary school teacher soon will end, allowing her still more time for many other interests, including antique collecting- from children's toys to Indian artifacts. And there always is the "social secretary" aspect, coordinating Don's guiding trips through phone calls and other contacts. Day to day guiding on the McKenzie has changed, Don says; there's almost no more fishing until dark, which lessens the strain on a marriage. Wouda:

"Long trips to other rivers, however, are hard on everyone. Wives hold the home together. Jiff (his name for Jennifer) senses that after several days on a river I'd just as soon stay home awhile as take her fishing, so she only gets out maybe once a year.

As a PE instructor, Wouda worked more with young groups. As a guide, often only one-on-one, he was able to observe and learn from adults. Don:

"As a guide, I had to learn to be both a teacher and a coach. A lot of clients, while owning nice equipment, have never used it much. Once neither the teaching or coaching efforts work, you have to evaluate what a client can do and work from there, putting them into water they can handle. And keep reminding myself who is doing the fishing!"

Seriousness aside, there are the refreshing exceptions, sometimes conducive to a bit of kidding around. Wouda:

"Dixie Monkhouse is an amazing person and an excellent fisherman, in spite of her fly-rod. That's something I like to tease here about, a seven-foot fiberglass almost as old as she is. She's actually quite good with it, even with big fish!"

Other memorable "dudes" Wouda leaves cloaked in anonymity, as follows:

Client One— "Broke his Powell rod, only one in our boat. He fished it, minus the handle and reel, hooking several big fish. I managed the reel, he managed the rod and line."

Client Two— "Broke his graphite rod. Splinted, it made casting and setting the hook interesting. It was raining and the fish were really coming."

(Since then, Wouda has always carried an extra rod.)

Client Three— "Keeps track of his fish with pennies. Starts day with two rolls of fifty each. Throws one in river each time he catches a fish. Keeps a written record as well. Has been coming twice a year, six days each time, for many years!"

Client Four— "Saves all the flies he uses each trip, keeping them in separate boxes for each trip. Has a special section for big fish flies— those fish 14 inches and over."

Client Five— "At 82 still comes twice a year for six days each, fishing for big fish only. When that's the only goal, you often are disappointed."

Clients Six & Seven— "The husband always came dressed in slacks and sport coat. His wife was equally well-dressed. They did this for years...."

Wouda also has some general observations on changing times:

"Thirty years ago, guides never offered chairs to their clients. In fact, old-time guides didn't and wouldn't use anchors or tables or chairs. Those are pretty standard now — even table clothes!"

He also notes that, as he has gotten older, he has begun to realize that while he is moving about enough to still be comfortably warm on the river during early spring or late fall trips, his guests may not be. As a result, he has taken a propane heater more than once. Wouda:

"On occasion, it has saved the trip, at least made it more pleasant. That cold 1999 season-ender with Dixie, we had the heater I use for winter steelhead fishing. Think I am the only one who does this..."

Practicality also rules on dry hot summer days. During traditional noon fish frys, when fire closures are in effect, a propane stove is utilized rather than a wood fire with its pungent fragrance.

"Those butter-fried trout," Wouda assures, "still taste just as great!"

BLUE RIVER—When the world's trout fishermen talk of Oregon, they think about its king of rivers, the Rogue, and its queen, the Deschutes.

But the aristocracy is incomplete with outside glimpses at Prince Umpqua and the princess of all rivers—the delicate, delectable and deceptive McKenzie.

Flushed from a lake famed for its clarity and embraced for nearly its entire route by an emerald canopy, the McKenzie passionately tumbles and muscles its way out of the Cascade Mountains over stones, pebbles and boulders easily visible in even the deepest blue-green holes.

Her kisses on the skin of a boat or raft are alternately tender and temperamental. Soft, billowing currents often erupt into white-water fury as the river bends and dives, scrambling to catch up with its wayward downhill path.

The watery highway leaves indelible memories.

—Bill Monroe

THE OREGONIAN, 9 July 1982

JOHN SHELLEY WEST

JOHN SHELLEY WEST
1901-1986

Fifty-eight years as a professional river guide earned John West legendary status among his peers. Last of the nine charter members of the McKenzie River Guides Association, he was a guide's guide, teaching his craft to younger river men and McKenzie-style fly fishing to novice clients. When the guides association was formed in 1931, West already was a seasoned journeyman with eleven years of running the McKenzie behind him.

Navigation on the McKenzie then often was tentative. Portages were arranged around the more formidable challenges, especially Martin Rapids, first navigated by Carey Thomson, jr., in 1925. The famed McKenzie drift boat had not yet evolved. West had learned river running in klunky old boats made out of heavy planks.

Dave Helfirich, now senior in the Prince Helfrich guiding dynasty, remembers West:

"He said, 'when you went through some rapids in those days, you'd run 'em with just one oar in the water. You'd have a bailing can in the other hand.' "West said, 'you never could use both oars in white water because you were bailin' all the time!' "

As a result, West had serious interest in evolvement of a more river-worthy craft, and contributed modification suggestions toward the ultimately classic McKenzie river drift boat of today. West had seen all the McKenzie offered by the time lung cancer forced him into semi-retirement. He had boated political, business and entertainment celebrities. Some clients were the third generation of their families, still being taught subtleties of fly fishing McKenzie redsides. Even in "retirement" West's trademark pith helmet set him apart as he continued to be seen behind the oars—just for personal pleasure—on yet other rivers—Deschutes, Rogue, Salmon, Snake and Alsea. But the McKenzie was his lifetime favorite. River life there was his life.

TUCK AND WADE THOMAS

"New kids on the block" must pay their dues before becoming accepted regulars, especially when peers are the tight circle of professional McKenzie River guides. Few, if any, have ever "graduated" into those seasoned ranks more deftly than Wade Thomas. Who, in turn, defers to his wife and partner, Tuck.

How they succeeded, in spite of the challenges arising from their other career paths, is a remarkable testimonial to focus and persistence reinforcing natural aptitudes. They were young marrieds from Boise Valley in Idaho, come to coach and to teach at McKenzie School in the year 1967. Wade had farm boy fishing background, but the McKenzie was a new challenge. Wife Tuck:

Dan Callaghan photo

"Wade bank fished and waded and for four years bounced in and out of sheer elation and frustration. He talked to many old-timers and realized the way to fish the McKenzie was from a boat. A teacher friend and Wade together bought an old Woodie Hindman boat and got it shipshape again."

Multiple school duties assured the path to Wade's ultimate goal to enjoy moonlighting as a river guide would be a long one. Coaching football was just a start. As athletic director he also either coached or had to be available for all other sports, plus driver's ed. He was lucky to have brief summer months for guiding. In contrast, upon leaving education in 1997, after thirty years, his guiding time more than doubled.

That he left his mark on McKenzie School's athletic history is perpetuated in a prominent sign of dedication, "WADE THOMAS FIELD." Just as that honor was thirty years a building, his select clientele of today simply didn't happen overnight. The Thomas' choice of an upriver neighborhood was fortuitous, and their engaging personalities assured them key friendships among an important California group of fly-fishing and golfing enthusiasts. Tuck:

"When Wade's parents left their Idaho farm, we got them caretaking jobs at the grand summer home of then Pauline and Marshall Fisher. After Marshall's death, Pauline—one of the original old-time fly-fishing goddesses of the McKenzie—married Allen Chickering, another icon river visitor. Pauline and yet other summer neighbors, Louise and Baltzer Peterson and Dixie and Reg Monkhouse, Jacque and Carlton Coveny introduced Wade to their then favorite guides—Frank Brown and Ennis Nestle. And, as those guides became older and retired, Wade was a logical replacement."

During those years, another family friend, Butch Taylor, introduced Wade to yet another icon guide, Merl "Mac" McMullin. Gradually, the Thomases became part of The Establishment. And, in no small measure due as well to the force which Tuck became along the river! Once leaving her second grade teaching job to have daughter Amy, Tuck launched incredible careers of volunteerism beyond her substitute teaching and all sport involvements, including Little League.

She helped start a nursery school still in operation today, worked with the Lane County health nurse to set up baby "well clinics," vaccination clinics, fulfilled some of the seniors' needs, ran parenting classes, etc. Tuck:

"That was all we had up here, medical-wise, when our children were small. Once the McKenzie River Medical Clinic became a reality, I served on the board and as a veep for two years. When Wade, Jr, was an eighth grader and Amy was in the eleventh grade, we moved into Eugene so they could have bigger school experiences. That was the beginning of the long, horrible commute back to McKenzie School and guiding for Wade, Sr."

The commute has eased, with the Thomas' now in a river cottage in the Walterville area near Holiday Farm.

Tuck was just warming up in the medical arena, first volunteering at Sacred Heart Hospital and then employed for seven years at Lane County Medical Society. From medical she switched to legal, volunteering to work with victims of sexual or physical assault, homicide or other crimes against person—helping them through their traumatic experiences and the legal maze.

For personal recreation Tuck turns to skiing—water, snow and cross-country. She became scuba certified at age fifty, and at same age made a dream free fall of 10,000 feet during a parachute jump.

She likes jammin' to New Orleans style jazz. On the more sedentary side, she has turned from jogging to walking and is getting back to golf. Is a family fishing dynasty a building?

Under his father's ongoing tutelage, Wade, Jr., is becoming an expert boatman. He was given his father's prize wooden Keith Steele drift boat when he turned 29 in '99. Dad retains another wooden Steele and, in step with a trend on the river, recently bought an aluminum craft. Tuck:

"At this point, Son Wade is an adrenaline junkie and prefers to row the challenging white water. I do see him fly-fishing more in the future. Daughter Amy did fish in her younger years, but now has a thing about killing fish."

And Tuck herself as an angler?

"Ahhh yes, very occasionally—for, as you know, my personal guide is almost always busy!"

McKENZIE RIVER GUIDES ASSOCIATION

The year was 1931, a time of testing America's mettle, three decades before the Flyfishers Club of Oregon was formed in the by-then prosperous Portland. But back then, times were tough and getting tougher as the Great Depression tightened its grip. In the McKenzie Valley, locals were eating deer meat more often than beefsteak.

Many were used to adversity and, naturally, drew closer together for their mutual benefit. And so it was in 1931 that a few adventurous rivermen gathered and formed the McKenzie River Guides Association. Besides the four Thomsons—Dayton, Milo, York and Carey, Jr.—there were Prince Helfrich, Rube Montgomery and his son, Howard, and the West brothers, John and Roy.

They had common concerns related to their then mostly seasonal guiding careers. Sometimes, for extra income, they manned trout planting boats for the state. And of that sideline Prince Helfrich once explained how they resisted the temptation of planting fish in some of their favorite waters:

"We don't put them (trout) in our own secret little pockets ... we distribute them right down the middle of the river!"

After the 14-inch trout restriction was imposed, guides as a group kept records. At the program's start, guides were reporting, collectively, as few as ten large rainbow trout caught and released during the season.

Within the decade, the number jumped to fifty and then towards one hundred! Those fish were spawners, contributing to a growing population of catch-and-release trout.

When their clients seemed agreeable, guides in the main also worked toward catch-and-release attitudes about fly-fishing. They demonstrated the ease and benefits of that method, and hoped for an official movement in that direction. Today, catch-and-release is the rule on native trout whose fins have not been clipped.

The association devised an Honorary Membership certificate to be awarded anyone catching and releasing a trout of 14 or more inches. Dedicated anglers acquired an imposing number of what some guides called "Paper Trout." So much so that the certificates now are given only if the angler has earned and wants one.

Most remembered about the guides group is what began as pre-season reconnaissance of river conditions but grew to unmanageable proportions. At first, guides made a safety check to learn how winter/spring runoff had changed the McKenzie's currents, eddies and possibly presented new obstruction challenges. They then updated their drift boat strategies accordingly. Wives and other family members were invited, as were some favorite clients.

Gradually, the combination work/play string of boats increased to parade proportions. Over time, the river inspection took a backseat to the sociability aspects. A community dance was added, ahead of the parade, increasing the event's popularity. By word of mouth and press reports, the parade grew just like Topsy. Ted Bryant, forty-year river veteran, remembers:

"At its peak, the parade was made up of anywhere from 600 to 900 various and often unworthy floating craft, including bathtubs! It had become unmanageable and dangerous!"

When the parade was discontinued officially in 1968, a EUGENE REGISTER-GUARD headline told the story. Under a sub head, "It's too big to handle," the headline read OVERPOPULARITY KILLED WHITE WATER PARADE.

Perhaps even more than sheer size of the parade, the recklessness of many occupants contributed to the end. Many craft were manned by "kegger" students from nearby University of Oregon. Some celebrated to excess, giving beer six-packs priority space over steering oars and life jackets.

Guides priorities shifted from river checking for their own safety to rescuing upended tagalongs from dangerous McKenzie waters. Traditional family picnics became a casualty. Dave Helfrich describes conditions toward the end:

"Finally, a lawyer told us that we, as original sponsors, had our necks out a foot! Even though we were patrolling all the dangerous spots and checking to see if everyone had life jackets, we would be responsible for parade boating accidents.

"Leroy Pruitt and I finally used power boats to make quicker trips to trouble spots. We'd run out and get 'em, take 'em to safety ashore, then run back up river to get the next one!"

Keith Steele, talented boat builder who presided for the last eight years of the parade's turbulent 30-year life, remembered that the first twenty years were relatively care-free. Then came the Sixties, and the rowdy crowds. Steele:

"People aren't the same anymore. They don't care. There's no consideration. I'm embarrassed by the things that go on in this parade now. I'll be damned if I ever have anything to do with another one!"

And so ended a tradition begun with prudent safety concerns, but evolving—partly because of national media exposure—into the prime elements of a crowded, boisterous accident just waiting to happen.

Without the sponsorship, expertise, and vigilant stewardship of river guides, the inevitable did happen. There were two drowning deaths in 1969, another in 1970, and one related fatality on McKenzie River Highway.

Long gone now are the trash heaps littering riverbanks, roadsides, lawns, orchards and fields. Today only mixed memories remain of the once celebrated annual White Water Parade.

CHAPTER 3

DRIFT BOATS

DRIFT BOAT HISTORY

BY ROGER FLETCHER

THE PREACHER & THE PRINCE

The air is so still, the only sounds are those of labored breathing, muffled grunts and an occasional "Careful!" or "Watch your step!" The year is 1928. The location is a patch of old growth timber. Their destination is about three miles up the Smith, a McKenzie River tributary. Travel is by foot. In order of priority, their gear includes heavy doses of ambition, a 13-foot board-and-batten boat and oars, one fly rod, creel and assorted flies. They share one bedroll to keep the weight down, a frying pan and lard and considerable energy. Additional gear is stashed at the confluence of the Smith and the McKenzie to support the remainder of their odyssey.

The Preacher, Leroy Pruitt, left, and the Prince, Prince helfrich, as seconds in the 1939 movie, "Abe Lincoln of Illinois."

Who are these men? Why would they hand-haul a boat through road-less timber and brush to launch it? Was it because few people had ever fished the Smith and visions of dancing native cutthroat captured their imagination? Was it because the Smith was simply a new stream to run? Or, was it to experience, first hand, an environment unadulterated by man? I suppose they were drawn by all three. In retrospect, the legacies left by these men and their peers were pioneering. The two people who could answer my questions are gone. I can imagine myself sitting around a campfire at river's edge, under panoplies of stars, discovering just what made them tick. They were the Preacher and the Prince, Veltie Pruitt and Prince Helfrich.

They had met a year earlier. One was a trained geologist and professional fishing guide whose concerns about environmental issues were ahead of his time. A University of Oregon graduate, he returned to his McKenzie home grounds to engage in his passion—the river. The other was a licensed preacher, fisher of men and trout whose love of the river's touch regularly drew him to the McKenzie from his home in Eugene. Both had earlier plied the McKenzie in the heavily timbered, cumbersome riverboats used by sports fishing locals and guides of the day. They were frequently referred to as "the old scow," a heavy duty, flat bottom skiff of limited freeboard and reasonable stability in calm water. In flowing water it was awkward, in heavy white water the skiff was troublesome. For the foolhardy, however, this boat provided access to the many pockets of fish on the water. Shallow riffles and arduous white water such as Martin Rapids demonstrated the limitations of this boat, yet the "old scow" served its users with modest satisfaction from the late nineteenth century through the 1920s.

Dallas Murphy (left) and Charles Harold Richards in the 'old scow', 1917.

Frustrations with the "old scow" drew the Preacher and the Prince together by chance. Obviously they were not dragging a 22-foot behemoth through the timber to launch on the Smith. Indeed, their boat was a light 13-foot square-ender built by the Preacher. The 1/4" x 12" strakes and 1/2" x 12" bottom boards were old growth spruce. Construction was board and batten. Seams were caulked with pitch, tar and cotton yarn. The frames were constructed of Port Orford cedar.

The boat measured three feet across the bottom amidships and five feet across the sheer, just large enough to accommodate two men and light gear, yet small enough to portage easily. There appears to have been a modest rocker (upward rake under the stem and stern) of the bottom, allowing for very quick pivots and pulls on the oars in busy water. Interior appointments were limited to bench seats, one for the oarsman and one for the partner. A fly-line deck is not visible in Veltie's first boat but he soon added what appears to be a handhold and shinbrace to aid in standing.

The Preacher's boat may not have been the first alternative to replace the "old scow" style skiffs of the McKenzie but it was, according to Veltie's son, Leroy, the first light boat. McKenzie River men such as John and Roy West built board and batten boats with broad, square sterns by the early to mid-1920s. The West's boats, while lighter and much more versatile than the

Veltie Pruitt's car top boat, the light board and batten McKenzie, circa 1930.

longer, heavier skiffs of the day still required a trailer. Veltie Pruitt's boat was small enough to be placed on a rack that straddled a touring car. It was also light enough to portage a couple miles through uncharted country river's edge and versatile enough for a skilled oarsman to dance and pirouette down technically difficult streams.

Veltie fly fishing off the stern of his first light board and batten boat, circa 1926.

The Preacher built his first light riverboat in about 1925. One day in 1927 as Veltie plied the McKenzie, he was hailed over to the bank by a guide with a "dude." The guide was Prince. He had seen Veltie and his boat a couple of times on the river. Prince introduced himself and inquired about the boat. Being a Pruitt I imagine Veltie invited Prince to "take it out and row it around a bit." Prince did. He liked it and asked Veltie to build such a boat for him. Thus began a lifetime friendship that engaged those drift boating pioneers, and some others, with a variety of rivers. The Prince and the Preacher pioneered the Smith, Crooked, Metolious, upper Rogue, Deschutes and John Day Rivers—all in Veltie built boats.

"The Preacher and the Prince" at the end of their famous pioneering down the Deschutes in Veltie's boat, 1938.

Press Pyle, a respected Rogue River guide, had the opportunity to "row a 13-foot boat from Grants Pass to Gold Beach" in the late 1930s. Pyle does not identify the boat owner but he does report it as a McKenzie, and:

"It bobbed like a cork! Sat real high in the water, it did. It would kind of skitter. Scared the hell out of me! Took me places on that river I never been before. I never rowed one again." (from a taped interview with Steve Prichett). But, later in his life Pyle apparently did row a 12-footer. Bobbie Pruitt of Grants Pass talked Pyle into rowing the smaller square-ender on a guided Owyhee River trip in Southeastern Oregon sometime after 1953.

Veltie abandoned board-and-batten construction in 1939 after he and Prince saw a plywood square-ender built by Tom Kaarhus the summer before. The encounter was during the filming of Abe Lincoln in Illinois, in which the twosome served as "extras." Leroy Pruitt recalls his dad and

A "bathtub with oarlocks," with Woodie Hindman at Gate Creek Rapids on the McKenzie, circa 1935.

Prince commenting that the Kaarhus design would make "a great white water boat." After the Preacher converted to the plywood boat he gave away his two remaining board-and-batten boats—one to his good friend Dallas Murphy, who continued to use the boat into the 1940s, frequently with Veltie's son, Leroy, at the oars. The second boat he gave to Maude Rogers. She lived at Pringle Falls on the Deschutes and was a Pruitt and Helfrich family friend.

Thus began a tradition of McKenzie River drift boats that today are revered around the world. The Preacher and the Prince symbolize the ingenuity resident in other early McKenzie guides such as Carey Thomson, Rube Montgomery, John and Roy West and others who vied for boats that were functional, versatile and safe. More important, those boats brought them and their clients to the river's touch.

A Son of Norway

Walter Siebolt and Howard Hall of the Kaarhus Craft Shop, circa 1935.

One opinion suggests that Carey Thomson started it all when he began to guide for hire on the McKenzie in 1909. (Lane County Historian, Vol. XXIX, No. 1, David Rodrigues). Soon men like Bill Price and Rube Montgomery began guiding for hire. Others followed suit. The somewhat subtle drainage of the McKenzie allowed the cumbersome skiffs to serve a purpose for a while.

They were hauled to and from the river by horse and wagon.

Soon, however, guides were adapting their boats to fit their needs. Several built their own boats, each tweaking his design to his personal preference. John and Roy West may have been the first to build a driftable boat shorter than sixteen feet. Milo Thomson reportedly described the West boat as 'a bathtub with oarlocks" and questioned the wisdom of such a contraption. However, the shorter boat proved capable of traversing water the more heavily timbered skiffs couldn't manage. The "bathtub with oarlocks" was a curious yet effective change from the "old scow" and it seems to have set the stage for some of the later boats. Tom Kaarhus referred to his square-ender as the "John West boat."

Young Torkel "Tom" Gudmund Kaarhus, circa 1923.

The lighter, shorter board and batten boats were as various as the men who built them. Often the availability of materials governed the appearances of the "bathtubs with oarlocks." For example, some boats were constructed with four-inch strakes and floor timbers, while other builders were able to acquire ten- or twelve-inch material. I suspect the boats that proved most desirable were those with the strakes of greater width. Think about it. Weight and ease of handling became a priority in the evolution to unique McKenzie River drift boat characteristics.

Drift boat bottoms were built with more rocker fore to aft but were flat across. Bottoms measured from three- to four-feet amidships and five- to six-feet across at the sheer.

The stern or down river end remained square but was heightened and flared a bit to minimize splash. There was also increased flare to the sides to improve stability. Interior appointments were being added to accommodate some of the unique features of fly-fishing: leg braces for standing upright and fly line deck to catch and hold stripped line, for example. The evolution of the earliest McKenzie River boats was logical but probably unplanned. Basic rules of form and function were at work.

Harvey Denham, Adena Kaarhus (Tom's wife) and Everett Eggliston in a Kaarhus square-ender.

Although many had a hand in the evolution of these early boats, one person stands out as having popularized the emerging square-ended style. He was Torkel Gudmund "Tom" Kaarhus (pronounced "car-hoose") a Son of Norway. Born on a southwestern coastal island of Norway in 1893, by 1923 he had made his way to McKenzie River country, developing his trade skills enroute. He could craft functional boats, skis and furniture. He is remembered in Eugene as conductor and director of church and Sons of Norway

Veltie Pruitt building his first plywood boat from a Kaarhus kit, 1939.

choirs. After early years in a planing mill he began building boats for guides. It was Kaarhus who milled the spruce planks for Veltie Pruitt's first light riverboat.

Kaarhus loved rivers and both he and his wife, Adena, loved to fish. However, their favorite rivers were the Umpqua and the Deschutes. Yet his extraordinary woodworking and boat building skills would impact most greatly the drift boats of the McKenzie.

Opening the Kaarhus Craft Shop in 1935, he built and sold drift boats. His joinery skills with red cedar and Philippine mahogany in assembling parts for his McKenzie drift boat reduced but never fully overcame leakage inherent in board and batten construction.

In my view, Kaarhus' most significant contribution to the McKenzie was that of being an early adapter. He was one of the first to take advantage of plywood and waterproof glue, doubling his production from two boats to one over board and batten. He continued to use battens for a period as bottom skid runners. Plywood made boat modifications easier for guides' preferences. Kaarhus often called on Prince Helfrich for opinions on design.

Tom Kaarhus' son Joe (center) with a new Kaarhus built double-ender with a transom, circa 1950.

He turned his boats into wonderful dual-purpose watercraft with another adaptation — modifying the rocker and adding a removable plate to the stern transom. This accepted a motor much better than the newly innovated double-ender and made the boat at home on lake or river!

There is an unsolved mystery associated with this boat. In the early Fifties, Science & Mechanics published two detailed articles referring to this "original McKenzie River drift boat" as the "Rapid Robert." Yet today, while this craft remains widely known as the Rapid Robert, there is no solid clue as to how it came by that name. My guess is that Kaarhus' far-ranging sphere of influence — when he and his son, Joe Jr. built lake-skiffs, day-sailors and at least one trimaran — had something to do with it.

I like to think of Tom Kaarhus as the Henry Ford of the drift boat industry.

His unique ability to supply boats in a timely manner had, through the Forties, generated a growing demand beyond that of professional guides. The availability of square-enders increasingly made rivers available to more adventurous anglers. Guides no longer were sole proprietors.

The Kaarhus genius found additional expression by addressing interests of the do-it-yourselfers. In the late Thirties, he offered patterned drift boat kits, selling them to guides, white water fans and anglers alike. Veltie Pruitt built his first plywood drift boat in 1939 from a Kaarhus kit. Veltie's son, Leroy, utilized a Kaarhus kit in 1944 to build his first boat.

Ruth on the oars during the White Water Parade (circa 1940). Ruth was an accomplished guide and oarsman. The decked boat was built for her by Woodie.

Tom Kaarhus was a legend in his own time. His granddaughter, Maurya Kaarhuss, recalls his pointing out the boats he had built as they encountered them in a drift of the McKenzie together before his death in 1964. While remembered for a variety of contributions — fine homes, fine cabinetry, day-sailors and lake-skiffs, he is most remembered among the professional guiding community as the boat builder who popularized the square-ender.

Woodie Hindman

As McKenzie River guides explored other northwest rivers, one anomaly of the square-enders became apparent. It remained for a transplanted Texan to help remedy the problems troubling even deft oarsmen in heavy white waters.

Ruth tending camp on the Middle Fork, circa 1940.

To partially avoid the challenge with existing craft, boatmen learned to angle into a heavy curl at 45 degrees, the boat's downstream corner cutting through the wave. And the potential stall on a large curlback could be countered by hitting the wave with carry-through momentum.

Woodie Hindman (pronounced

hine-man) had been a Texas Panhandle ranch hand and cafe operator prior to his migration north to Eugene to lease a hotel. Shortly after arrival he became interested in the McKenzie, its fish and its riverboats. His spirit of adventure, sense of humor and talent as a camp cook were obvious. Less apparent initially were his insights as a gifted innovator.

In 1937 Woodie married Ruth Wilhoit who came to work in his hotel. It was a partnership in which she became equally adept at drift boat oars and they ran a number of rivers together. When Woodie was away on business and she needed a boating and fishing partner, she was often joined by Ruby Taylor, Kenny Taylor's wife.

The author's model of Woodie's first double-ender.

Woodie began his boat building career with Tom Kaarhus around 1935. By 1941 he had relocated to Springfield to build his own boat shop. It would be some time before his experiences of those early days would stir his innovative bent. Those exposures to the McKenzie and other rivers were with the popular Kaarhus style square-ender.

I had the opportunity in the spring of 2000 to capture the lines of a square-ender Woodie built in 1939. Frank Wheeler of Vida, OR, owns the boat. It is made of plywood and measures eleven feet, four inches stem to stern. Woodie built the boat for Prince Helfrich, who used it to run his winter trap lines on the McKenzie. It's a classic! Frank has a real treasure! The boat is the same as the one Woodie and Ruth used to run the Salmon's Middle Fork in August of 1939— the first successful solo of that river in a hard boat.

Quite naturally, Woodie and Ruth quickly became friends with the community of McKenzie River guides. The nucleus with whom they shared river adventures included Veltie Pruitt, Prince Helfrich, George Godfrey, Ed Thurston and Everett Spaulding. Godfrey, in addition to being a licensed McKenzie guide, was also a professor of journalism at the University of Oregon.

Woodie and Ruth, circa 1940.

Godfrey tells a story about Woodie and his square-ender on the Salmon's Middle Fork in August of 1939. Hindman's square-ender reportedly was slapped broadside in heavy water. Rather than fight the boat's pivot, he continued the swing of the boat, jumped from the rowing seat to the guest thwart (by one account just a bale of hay), and finished the rapid bow first. He liked the way the bow cut through the waves and tested the bow-first approach several times on that trip. John West in a 1975 Eugene Register-Guard story offers the same account. This is speculation on my part, but I suspect Woodie's experiences with the square-ender were cumulative and, given his innovative approach to problem solving, he had been thinking for some time about possible improvements to drift boats.

What we do know is that during the winter of 1939-40 Woodie built a double-ender. My study of the early boats indicates he essentially built a square-ender but instead of a large, flared transom he extended the natural lines to a down river prow. By modifying frames so fore and aft units matched, and by using flexible 3/8" plywood then available, he was able to craft the double-ender. His earliest double-ender was symmetrical fore and aft with a stern and stern post cut at 40 degrees to receive the side panels. The boat was about 13 feet long. Fourteen foot plywood panels were the longest available at that time.

Woodie (foreground) in his 16' double-ender and Kenny Taylor in a Woodie built double-ender with a transom, circa 1948.

The double-ended drift boat became an immediate hit. Its lines were swooping, elegant and functional. The profile view between stem and stern presented the most pronounced rocker among the original McKenzies. The lines of the sheer paralleled the bottom lines. The up-river end (bow) of the boat measured about fourteen inches from the base of the stem to the boat's base line. The down-river end measured about eleven inches in that area. In other words, the upward rake under the bow remained greater than the upward rake under the stern.

The double-ender became Woodie's personal favorite. There was, however, at least one limitation. The double prow reduced interior space, thereby making quarters more cramped for both client and gear. But for the oarsman, it was a gem to handle.

It was not until 1946 that Woodie introduced the double-ender to the Middle Fork. Sixteen foot plywood had become available and he was able to build boats of greater dimensions.

Guide Everett Spaulding, who was a double-ender man, takes credit, for

Woodie's next, and perhaps, most significant innovation:

"I was boating on the Umpqua, from the highway down to Kellogg and on down toward the ocean for salmon, trout and steelhead in August and September. The put ins and the take outs were far apart. We'd have to do a lot of rowing through those dead stretches. "

So I went to Woodie and I told him, "I want that bow chopped off!" He says, "Well, we'll ruin it!"

"I don't care if you do! I want it chopped off!" So, we chopped it off and put a motor on it so we could go through those dead stretches and save time." (as quoted in Dec. 14, 1974, Eugene Register-Guard.)

Another story, floating around the guiding community regarding Everett's intentions concerns his guiding for Glen Woolridge on the Rogue. His early trips went all the way to Lobster Creek, just above Gold Beach. He motored his boats the last thirty or so miles to reduce rowing time. Some say Everett had Woodie replace the bow with a transom just to keep up with Woolridge! Others believe that Woodie himself took note of motor use on the Rogue and modified his double-ender to test its utility.

Woodie (right) and Everett Spaulding and Everett's boat in the background, circa 1948.

Whatever the motivation, Woodie built a double-ender with a transom for Spaulding, and it became the standard for McKenzie River drift boats. The elegant swooping lines and the unique handling characteristics of the double-ender were retained. The small transom also enhanced interior space. While a motor assists movement through slow water, the boat's basic design does not lend itself to efficient use of such power. Such modification has, however, kept alive confusion and debate as to which end of the boat is the stern and which is the bow!

Several McKenzie guides continue to call this boat the double-ender, a name which seems to suggest her lovely lines, transportability, maneuverability and stability. Her dancing grace and quickness is the result of weight—a sixteen foot McKenzie can weigh less than 250 pounds! The significant rocker allows for quick pivots and pulls and the liveliness of her wood-based spirit.

THE REST OF THE STORY

Four original McKenzies as recovered and modeled by the author.

Another drift boat innovation generally credited to Woodie is the rowing thwart as a rope seat. That was welcomed for two features: first, allowing water to run off one's slicker and onto the flooring rather than puddling up and water-logging the oarsman's derriere, and also providing a comfortable and secure perch for the oarsman's bottom when the boat pitched in heavy water. However, Howard C. Hall, Kaarhus' first shop employee, says Kaarhus told of rope seats in dories when he fished commercially in Alaska. Hall claims Kaarhus placed rope seats in his early boats and Woodie simply adopted the idea.

There can be no doubt that guides such as Veltie Pruitt and Prince Helfrich and builders such as Tom Kaarhus and Woodie Hindman spawned the McKenzie River drift boat.

It then was up to men like Marty Rathje, Keith Steele, Tony Noe, Willard Lucas, Don Hill, Greg Tatman, John Ohstrum, Ray Heater and others to further refine and popularize the McKenzie. Each builder has added a personal stamp here and there, but the basic lines are of the Hindman double-ender.

In the face of increasing use of aluminum and fiberglass, only a very few quality wooden drift boat builders remain in McKenzie country. Bless each one of them! Anyone who has not danced with the river in a wooden McKenzie drift boat has not yet, in my opinion, experienced the full glory of the river's touch!

About the author: Roger Fletcher of Dallas, OR is an educator, author and craftsman who with his family has spent his lifetime on the river. He has been examining the origins of the McKenzie and Rogue River boats. His reincarnations of these early boats include detailed instruction plans and their re-creation as museum quality scaled models. For more information visit his web site www.riverstouch.com.

My Introduction to the McKenzie Drift Boat

By Lenox Dick, M.D.

In June 1947 my new father-in-law, Spencer Biddle was about to introduce me to the McKenzie River as we drove up the road that parallels the river. I saw an amazing sight and exclaimed, "Mr. B, I can't believe that man is rowing a boat up a rapid!"

Mr. B laughed and pulled the car over to the side of the road so we could watch.

He explained: "That man at the oars is a professional guide named Milo Thomson, an old-timer and one of the most famous guides on this river. Lenox, do you see that large rock about 30 feet above the boat. The rock splits the current and forms an eddy of quieter water downstream from it. The guide is holding the boat near the tail of the eddy as the angler casts his fly up close to the rock, where fish often hold. As the boat gets closer to the rock, the eddy current pushes the bow of the boat into the rock, and the angler then fishes just above the rock, where a large fish often holds in the cushion of current there. After Milo has worked all over the fishable water, he will turn the boat around and fish downstream. The boat you are watching is called a McKenzie River drift boat and was developed on this river for fishing just like that."

And so began my first fishing on that wonderful stream, which I have fished every year since.

Drifting in D.C.

Fame—as little as 15 minutes—leaves a mark on history's pages. When the national spotlight shines for an entire week on two chosen for their McKenzie expertise, the event is worth retelling here. This is the story of the late Keith Steele of Leaburg and of Ted M. Bryant of Eugene and their roles during Oregon Week 1976 Bicentennial Year celebrations in Washington, D.C.

When Congressman Jim Weaver tapped Steele, an acclaimed drift boat builder, as an Oregonian to participate in the American Folklife Festival, he in turn picked Bryant, popular river guide and fly dresser, to complete the McKenzie scene. Today, Bryant and wife, Ann, alone are left to recall, first hand, details of both public and behind-the-scenes adventures. Ted:

"My fly-tying and rod-building exhibits traveled well compared to Keith's. He made most boat parts—ribs, seats, etc,—here for air shipment to Washington. Not so the required sixteen-foot plywood sheets. Keith got eight-foot sheets in D.C. and spliced them. Eventually, we discovered we had no oars! Luckily, there were Oregon lumberjacks at high-climbing and log-rolling demonstrations to fashion a serviceable pair for us!"

The Steeles and the Bryants were flown to Washington, housed in dorms at nearby Georgetown University and, if they desired, took their morning and evening meals at the cafeteria there. They and all other Festival participants wore white badges to move freely about the congested area. Free busses shuttled between the university and festival grounds. Taxi fare then was only $2. Bryant:

"One of our regular McKenzie fishing clients, Trader Vic (Victor Jules Bergeron), did not visit our exhibits, but gave us a card good for dinner on him at his restaurant outlet in the nation's capitol. Keith and Loretta and myself and Ann — and several other couples — enjoyed that special night out!"

With few exceptions, the only recognizable visiting Oregonians the Bryants now remember were the timberjacks and the Indians demonstrating tribal dances and smoking fish. Congressman Weaver, of course, came by, as did Congressman Les AuCoin and Senators Hatfield and Packwood. President Ford drove by but didn't stop. Bryant:

"One of my first McKenzie clients, Neill Whisnant, made a special trip all the way from Oregon, stayed a couple days and spent some time casting from Keith's boat in the Reflecting Pool. He owned the Riverside Lodge that Keith and Loretta leased for their operation." (Whisnant, of Brady

Hamilton Stevedores, was a Oregon Flyfishers Club member until his death in 1993.)

Bryant also remembers yet another individual from among the faceless thousands who drifted by that week when he was demonstrating fly-casting from a float:

"He came along, watched awhile, then asked where he could get an outfit like mine, which would make one-hundred foot casts — for him!"

Besides a small per diem during their week's stay, the Bryants and Steeles were provided a charter flight home at conclusion of Oregon exhibitions.

Steele's drift boat stayed behind and, the story goes, continued on exhibition awhile longer. Recent inquiry, however, reveals no record of it becoming a permanent part of national museum collections. Is it possible the drift boat served out its useful life on the Potomac River?

Kieth Steele in bow, Ted Bryant at the oars.

Like that storied craft, both Keith and Loretta are missing from today's scene, but their McKenzie imprint continues in family members. Son Steve, a welding instructor at Lebanon H.S. turned naturally to building trailers for boats of his father and others. Son Stan, influenced by Uncle Bob Steele's fish-and-game warden career (featured elsewhere) also became a member of the state police force.

(With his sons help, Steele could put a boat together in a day, and he built approximately 2,000 during his relatively short career. His additional expertise and versatility are mentioned elsewhere.)

Ted and Ann Bryant still live in Eugene. Ted:

"I still boat with some of my friends and family, and I still make a few rods. Started boating when I was about 19 and got my first guide's license about three years after that — mostly to protect myself from some of my freeloader friends!"

Bryant got his first Hindman drift boat the same week his first son, Chuck, was born. Before becoming a guide, he took Chuck and young brother Jim both trout and steelhead fishing, almost every week, the latter to streams west of Eugene. Bryant:

"I had thought about living up the McKenzie, but Ann had her career bakery job in Eugene and also wanted to be closer to doctors' care for the kids' sake. Then, shorter trips to coastal steelhead streams made more sense during winter driving conditions."

The Bryant boys were ten and twelve, respectively, when Don Wouda, Chuck's PE teacher in middle school, started taking them fishing. Eventually, Bryant "conned him into guiding." (Wouda's story appears elsewhere.) Bryant:

"Chuck is a very good boatman and fisherman, but makes more at another job. Same with Jim. Our daughters like to fish, too, but it's the old story — the shoemaker's family who had no shoes...."

Bryant was between jobs in the spring 1963 when he decided to shift from weekend and vacation time guiding to fulltime — for that summer, at least but, as he explains:

"I just never got away from it!"

Chapter 4

Some of the Fishers

"A good fish for the McKenzie—dry fly—Leonard rod, guide Cecil Beyerlin."

Lee Richardson
1938

Hoover and the Iron Hat

Few, if any, would challenge that the most distinguished fly-fisherman ever on the McKenzie was the 13th president of this nation, Herbert C. Hoover. Not necessarily the most expert in his many, many visits but surely one of the most passionate, his words telling much more than his stoic appearance and demeanor.

In his Fishing For Fun — And To Wash Your Soul, Random House, 1963, Mr. Hoover wrote:

"When I was ten years old, I was transported to Oregon. Oregon lives in my mind for its gleaming wheat fields, its abundant fruit, its luxuriant forest vegetation, and the fish in the mountain streams. To step into its forests with their tangle of berry branches, their ferns, their masses of wild flowers, stirs up odors particular to Oregon. Within these woods are never-ending journeys of discovery, and the hunts for grouse and expeditions for trout."

Photo Courtesy of Herbert Hoover Presidential Library

President Hoover in uncharacteristic casual dress.

Young Hoover metamorphosed as an angler like most boys everywhere. He candidly admits:

"I, like other boys, fished with worms until a generous fisherman whom we met during an excursion to the upper Santiam, gave four of us three artificial flies each. They proved powerfully productive. It never occurred to me that they were perishable. In any event, I nursed those three flies and used them until all the feathers were worn off — and still the trout rose to them. The upper Santiam has sadly degenerated since.

"A brand-new fly of any variety, even carefully treated with cosmetics and attached to gut leaders and expensive rods, has nothing like the potency of that bamboo pole with fly tied directly upon the end of a string."

Details of those decades of fishing while shifting from a Newberg, OR, family home address to the White House are sketchy. When Secretary of Commerce, Hoover in 1928 visited Portland, surely with side trips to Newberg and the McKenzie. His colorful ex-stunt pilot, Forest Myrten "Iron Hat" Johnston also flew Mr. Hoover and his son, Herbert, Jr., to Salem where, among other ceremonies he was presented an over-sized box of cigars as "The Engineer of the Century." (Johnston was dubbed "Iron Hat" by fellow daredevil pilots in the post-World War I era because he seldom was without his hard English derby and had Chaplinesque mannerisms. He often was part of Mr. Hoover's fishing party.) Mr. Hoover returned again to Newburg in August 1955, on his 81st birthday for ceremonies dedicating the restored family home.

"I come to the McKenzie River for a brain-washing and to refresh my soul," former president Hoover told a reporter of the Eugene Register-Guard in 1956 when he was on one of his frequent vacations at the Holiday Farm Resort at Rainbow. From 1932 to 1958, the late president visited the resort two or three times a year, seeking solitude and the occasional splash of a trout at the end of his line.

There are disparate assessments of Mr. Hoover's expertise as a fly-fisherman.

Those in the best position to know after guiding him on river drifts—chief among them Fred Harris, John West, and Prince Helfrich—also are gone. Marjorie Helfrich had clear memories of Prince discussing fishing tips with Mr. Hoover.

No doubt they would've been too diplomatic to be negative. It was, however, a distinct honor to have him in one's boat. The late great guide, Merl "Mac" McMullin, who had Standard Oil's president in his drift boat during Mr. Hoover's 82nd birthday party on the McKenzie, once observed:

"Now that President Hoover is gone, a lot of McKenzie guides remember him as their client!"

One of the most critical of Mr. Hoover's angling prowess was Col. Edmund Starling, head of the White House detail protecting five presidents (Woodrow Wilson to Franklin D. Roosevelt). In his Starling of the White House, Simon & Schuster, 1946, he wrote:

"As a fisherman the President knew what he was doing when trolling from a boat or fishing downstream with a wet fly. When it came to casting upstream with a dry fly he was out of his class."

Col. Starling appears to be a bit over his waders himself. He claimed to have helped Mr. Hoover's fly-fishing techniques. But Dr. William P. Allan, curator at Stanford University's Cecil H. Green Library, says Starling helped Calvin Coolidge fly-fish — not Hoover — for the resultant publicity.

Dr. Allan:

"As I recall, he claims he taught Hoover how to fish; a claim I rather doubt."

Hoover himself supports Allan's surmise in his Fishing For Fun comments in describing President Coolidge's progressing from common worming for trout, when his public expected more:

"Then Mr. Coolidge took to a fly. He gave the Secret Service guards great excitement in dodging his back-casts and rescuing flies from trees."

Mr. Hoover was correct at the time he wrote the following:

"President Theodore Roosevelt, President Cleveland and myself— with a slight egotism! — I think were the only Presidents who had been lifelong fly-fishermen before they went to the White House."

At the time, Mr. Hoover's friend, Dwight D. Eisenhower, was still a general, not a president, but was advancing from an angler of common fish to fly-fishing — a certain sign, Mr. Hoover surmised, he was becoming a presidential candidate. Since then, Jimmy Carter has joined the ranks of fly-fishing presidents.

❧❧❧

Fishing, it turned out, was a family affair for the Hoovers. A granddaughter, Mrs. Margaret Hoover Brigham, West Chester, PA, in 1997 wrote Creel editors as follows:

"My fishing memories of my grandfather start when he good-humoredly furnished me with some sort of pole and line and let me drop it in his favorite pool at Rapidan Camp in Virginia. He didn't think, at age three, I was much of a threat to his pet trout (large)! What still stays with me is that suddenly he was taking my first catch off the hook, and throwing it back. I was devastated!

"Due to school obligations I only had sporadic opportunities to fish with him; steelhead fly-fishing once. Later, when at college on the East Coast, I was able to join him during vacation in the Florida Keys, bone fishing ... which he loved.

"My parents joined him to keep him company and enjoy the ambiance that fishing provided ... the out-doors and the people that were with him.

"Fishing gave him the rare and valued moments to be alone ... moments that combined action and meditation! It refreshed him! It was a chance to study the lay of the water, plan an approach, and pit his long-acquired knowledge against his quarry. The majority of the time, he would toss the fish back, unless it was a particularly large or tasty one. He was not one to boast of his take.

"I'm sorry I have no pictures ... there are few situations where privacy is more valued than when fishing, and that includes the intrusion of cameras."

Chief Justice William O. Douglas, in review for the National Wildlife Federation, describing Mr. Hoover as "... a model Izaak Walton ... admitted that while he never fished with the 13th president, ... we shared some exciting spots.

"Those who know these stretches of water can point out places famous because President Hoover fished there." (While no strictly Hoover waters are known to exist today on the McKenzie, the name lives on at a Holiday Farm cottage called Hoover House. Vivienne Wright, former Holiday Farm owner-operator, says the Hoover family used it until lives of members took different paths. After that, into the Sixties, Mr. Hoover used a smaller waterside cottage at Holiday Farm. —Editor)

In the Herbert Hoover Library, West Branch, Iowa, repose Mr. Hoover's lunch box and pillows (seat cushions) used by him on McKenzie fishing trips. They were given by "Hard Hat" Johnston.

Some large fish weren't released.

Senior archivist at the Hoover library, Dwight M. Miller, in 1997 speculated that Johnston should have many stories to tell. However, "Hard Hat' had died three years earlier.

Mr. Hoover was an active champion of more hatchery production to meet the growing demand for a diminishing resource. In The Memoirs of Herbert Hoover, The Cabinet & The Presidency, 1920-1933, MacMillan Co., 1952, Chapter 22, "An Interlude—Fishing," he warned:

" ... we lose ground every year, sector by sector, as the highways include more fishing holes in the route ... it is too long between bites; we must have

years and made some remarkable catches. I well remember seeing some Caddis and Red Upright hatches that made these pools boil with large fish!"

That pristine circumstance deteriorated when the Depression days of the early Thirties, brought CCC camp workers who built a road into it.

Soon accessible by automobile to what Witter termed "bait and spinner boys," the pools were quickly ruined. Witter:

"There was one pool at the foot of a waterfall that had been especially beautiful. ...Vincent Whitney and I fished there one day and found few fish and a lot of empty salmon egg bottles and other debris left by those who believe that catching fish is an end worthwhile in itself and that the means are unimportant."

In spite of the desecration there, they caught several trout of about a pound each on big, white bucktailed Royal Coachmen, fished dry. Witter:

"In order to present my own fly properly I had to climb up on a dead limb, projecting out from a dead tree. It was rather precarious casting, but quite effective. Apparently the bait boys had been unable to reach some parts of the pool."

Witter found accommodations at Buck Travis' place, above McKenzie Bridge, better suited to his style, commenting "... we lived like kings there." However, nothing is perfect, as Witter explains:

"One morning John went into the kitchen to make some dry-fly oil by dissolving paraffin in ether. Both he and the cook were partially asphyxiated by the fumes and left the kitchen in great alarm. Thereafter we mixed our dry-fly oil out of doors."

Witter's father had exposed him to the fishing itch when he was just a lad on their modest vineyard south of Cloverdale, in northern Sonoma County. Then it was a jumping off place for horse and springwagon trips to streams west and north.

He remained active even when he no longer made the exhausting auto trips required because Coleman never ever drove. Luckily, Witter could pull off the road and, after forty winks, be rarin' to go again. There came a time, however, when he had to be chauffeured. Daughter Ann:

"I drove Dad to the hunting and fishing places in the Sixties, when he was in his seventies. Dad got sick in the fall of 1963 when we did our first Helfrich trip down the McKenzie. My daughter, Cody, then sixteen, substituted for Dad."

At the end, the strain of a full outdoor life of hunting and fishing, in addition to managing to grow Dean Witter & Co., into the biggest U.S. brokerage company outside of New York with 4,000 employees, 64 offices around the country and a net worth of $54 million took its toll. Dean Witter's heart simply failed him.

DIXIE MONKHOUSE

At first glance, Dixie Monkhouse strikes one as a very pretty and petite 90-year-old (in 1999). Engage her in conversation and you discover a grand lady with keen wit and firm resolve and an abiding love for the McKenzie and her riverside "Monkabin" retreat.

Any fishing chat with Dixie eventually turns to her favorite outfit—a 2 ounce glass rod and Hardy reel bought for her by her late husband, Reginald, in 1959 at Abercrombie & Fitch, New York. Dixie:

"I've fished nothing else since then! Dad's bamboo Powells were too tiring when I used to wade and fish Horse Creek."

One of her early guides for twenty years, Ernest Nestle, is known to ask if Dixie's " … still fishing that rod?" Both of them recall a shared highlight when she played a steelhead while Nestle navigated them through Martin Rapids.

Dixie was born, raised and schooled in San Francisco where her father was a Crocker Bank executive. They first fly fished together on the upper Klamath River in Northern California. Dixie:

"Wet fly, you know, for regular steelhead only, a few miles below where the river road takes off from the freeway. There was an old lodge there that everybody knew. It was a great beginning!"

Early in the Fifties the Monkhouses came to the McKenzie, staying at Thomson's Lodge and fishing with Cecil Byerlin, and early-day guide. Byerlin lived across the river from Thomson's where a long flat is named after him. When Thomson's burned, the Monkhouses went to Holiday Farm. Dixie:

"That was a lucky move for us! Holiday Farm owners in 1955 were retiring and wanted to sell 800 of their 1,200 feet of river footage. Dad reminded us that riverfront property would only increase in value. So my husband and I acquired 400 front feet—and weren't charged for the cabin on it, which became Monkabin!"

The next Monkhouse guide was Fred Harris a big, quiet man and a good guide who was fond of drink and finally killed himself. Another old-time guide Dixie remembers is Ted Bryant. Dixie:

"He's still around (1999)! Every year he says he is going to retire from guiding. I don't know that he has, but he still is making beautiful graphite rods popular with other McKenzie guides."

When fishing with Nestle— "…a wonderful guide much admired by younger boatmen …" the supercargo always was one of three miniature poodles in the Monkhouse boat—for a period of 35 consecutive years.

(first "Monkey," then "Beppo," after a toy monkey that Reg had as a child, and finally "Shanti," Arabic for monkey.) Dixie:

"They were quite well-known on the river. We'd take their cushions and put them underneath shelving in Ennis' drift boat and they were as good as gold!"

One of Dixie's unique experiences with a "fishnapper" was duplicated by a nephew and member of our club, Garrett P. Scales. His descriptive account appeared in the club's February 1995 newsletter under the title, "A McKenzie Bonefish." It's worth reading.

In Dixie's case, Wade Thomas was the guide and Dixie was playing a modest-sized trout toward the drift boat. Dixie:

"WHAM! An osprey dove to grasp that fish and began climbing across the river with my fly line trailing behind. Wade broke it off, and that osprey flew across the river with my trout. He turned, came back over our boat and then on upriver. He was showing off!

Dan Callaghan photo

"I'll never forget that, nor will I forget my seven oversize (14" and over) trout which is the best I've ever done in one day. Guide Don Wouda had us way upriver, near the 'Fish Ladder' which is the only class IV rapid on the river. It is the only one where I am required to wear a life jacket, as does Don."

Annual McKenzie visits haven't always featured happy highlights. Dixie:

"Monkabin cabin was devastated in 1964, the flood just went all over and we had to replace all sorts of things. Then, in '96 we had another flood and it took off my porch. Since then it's been very hard to catch any fish over sixteen inches."

One of Dixie's favorite McKenzie stretches of the upper river is at Olallie Campground, also uppermost for put-ins. Dixie:

"It's a perfectly beautiful stretch of water! Then, I love to go with Wade Thomas to the South Fork of the McKenzie … actually the South Fork is above Cougar Dam and it's the stretch below Cougar Dam that we fish."

Prominently displayed on corner walls at Monkabin are old fishing hats, each with its memories. One her father bought years ago in Hawaii and Dixie sometimes fishes with it … and others belonged to her late husband ... yet another a gift from a river neighbor … and still another from Nephew Gary. Dixie:

"Others are just hats we wore when we had breakfasts on the porch in the sun."

Dixie doesn't keep planted trout for midday cookouts unless family or friends are in the party:

"I like to bring back just one 'planter' for myself and cook it with butter on both sides. The tails are like potato chips—they're the best part!

"That's a part of being on the river. Anytime on the river is a good time. Each late fall, when I leave for my winter home in San Rafael, CA, I leave a part of my heart on the McKenzie!"

Whitewater Baptism

By Ralph Wahl
1906—1996

History was being made when several hundred anglers meeting in Eugene in June of 1965, launched a national federation of fly-fishing clubs. Being able to mingle with Lee Wulff, Ted Trueblood, Ed Zern and other fly-fishing world writers was a treat. But my highlight was a personal first, whitewater river running. Northwest Washington's mighty Skagit had been my home river for much of my life. There, mostly, we waded for steelhead. And I was content to continue the practice—until fate decreed otherwise. The trip to Eugene from my Bellingham home was made with my Canadian friend, Tommy Brayshaw, and his charming Beckie. Tommy was just recovering from a serious heart attack, so my Jean and I took two days to drive to Eugene. During that drive, Tommy, an 80-year-old native yorkshireman steeped in the rich English angling tradition, fussed over what he would say to brother fly-fishermen. He was a panelist for "reflections and philosophies of fly-fishing" discussions. He needn't have worried. His link with the angling world's past, his old-country charm and keen wit captivated his audience. At the closing dinner of the three-day conclave, awards were given, mostly to celebrity participants. Tommy's was a free guided fishing trip down the McKenzie River. When we retired that night, Jean and I overheard a heated discussion in the Brayshaw's adjoining room. Next morning, Tommy, somewhat sheepishly, gave his trip ticket to me and insisted I go in his place. Turned out that Beckie wouldn't ok his floating the river.

Photo by Dan Callaghan

Gene Anderegg, first president of the aborning FFF, and I shared the high-bow McKenzie drift boat of our volunteer guide, Tom Warlick, Eugene optometrist. In a second boat, guided by Dr. Bill Gaughan, were two of my Washington State friends, Fran Wood and Sanford Bacon. They followed us ten miles upriver for boat launch and fishing. Four hours passed pleasantly, with some stops as the guides held us in good positions to fish likely trout waters. Each drift boat accounted for perhaps a dozen small rainbows.

They looked suspiciously like hatchery trout—just planted for our pleasure—not the famed McKenzie redsides. Thus continued our serene drift down river, until we reached the whitewater stretch called Martin Rapids. In fact, we had heard the booming water long before arriving there. Close up, that long stretch of tumbling white water, with its formidable standing wave, looked dangerous to me. On shore, our guides agreed to a passage plan—our boat would go first so we could get photographs of the others shooting the rapid. We stowed Anderegg's $2,000 leica and my beat-up Exakta cameras under a tarp, put on life vests, and were on our way. Our guide had promised a wet ride. It was! Our boat picked up speed and was soon in roaring white water. As it climbed the standing wave and crashed over the top, a sheet of water soaked us. Suddenly it was over, with Warlick easing us ashore near cabin-size boulders. With our cameras, Gene and I scrambled to the top of the highest one and signaled for the other boat to proceed. Their ride through Martin Rapids was even wilder than ours, with more water taken aboard, but it resulted in our getting some good photos. I often think of the truly historic accomplishments arising from that inaugural three-day conclave—and my baptism, literally, to whitewater boating!

Ralph Wahl's photo of a Martin Rapids run.

(Ralph Wahl wrote the above reminiscence Oct. 23, 1991. He is remembered for two classic books: Come Wade the River, Salisbury press, Seattle, 1971, combining Wahl's photographs and Roderick Haig-Brown's prose; and One Man's Steelhead Shangri-La, Frank Amato Publications, Portland, 1989.)

Gerstley and Friends

The McKenzie fly fishing and Tokatee golfing traditions of James M. Gerstley of Atherton, CA, ended abruptly in 1998 when he damaged his right shoulder. Before the reader's mind poses a "Too bad, but so what?" question, let Mr. Gerstley explain:

"By that time I was 92 and my wife some six years younger, but we will both always have wonderful memories of our times on the McKenzie."

Wonderful memories, indeed! Affording new insights into the way it was, beginning in the mid-Thirties. Gerstley, chief executive of the Borax Company of Twenty Mule Team fame for nearly a quarter-century, still speaks cogently and with clarity for an interesting group of family and friends. And it all began by sheer happenstance:

"Elizabeth and I were visiting her parents, the Lilienthals in Atherton, one weekend when my uncle, Harold Mack, a good friend of theirs, dropped by. Elizabeth, her father, and her brother were all good at fly fishing, as was Uncle Harold, so there was much conversation on that subject."

Gerstley had done very little flyfishing up to that time, but had so enjoyed it he and his wife accepted his uncle's invitation to his place on the McKenzie that very summer of 1937. Gerstley:

"Uncle Harold owned a very nice farm across the Leaburg Dam bridge, including a comfortable house and some cottages. He spent enough time there to become well known along the river and to make a contribution to fishing lore there."

Mack noticed a color variation in a fly hatch one season and got his guide to tie an imitation of the insect. Named the Mack Special, the pattern was widely used on the McKenzie at appropriate hatch times, according to Gerstley.

Mack's place was just upriver from the ultimately famous Thomson Lodge, and he befriended that family by making his farm cabins available to them as overflow lodging when not otherwise occupied. He suggested the Gerstleys get in touch with Dayton or Milo Thomson for their first McKenzie experience. Milo was available. Gerstley:

"We had never boated a river with rapids before and had to learn some new techniques. Eventually we caught a few fish, but the great enjoyment was sighting ospreys, beaver, black bear, some deer and different waterfowl.

Roger Schaad photo

"On subsequent trips with Milo, we wondered why he would go ashore every half hour or so. Later, we found out that he had bottles of liquor hidden in the woods near the river and apparently refreshed himself with frequent libations!"

A day's outing with Prince Helfrich afforded the Gerstleys with several new experiences, including the then still new McKenzie River tradition of a midday trout fry on the beach. Gerstley:

"Those butter fried trout were delicious! Prince was the first boatman to introduce such lunches on the river, and it later became part of the guide's responsibility. With other guides in those early days we brought our own lunch, usually sandwiches."

Another Helfrich highlight for the Gerstleys was when Prince stood up in a rough part of Martin Rapids to point out a water ouzel nest on a high rock in the river. Gerstley:

"When we started fishing the McKenzie, a boating guide charged $7 for half a day and $10 for a full day, which seemed quite a lot at my then modest salary.

(Gerstley had taken a job at U.S. Borax & Chemical Corp. in 1933, when times were lean. He became president of the corporation in 1950 and retired in 1962.) He continues:

"We also fished a lot with Cecil Byerlin, a most likeable and helpful guide. In 1938 he pointed out Herbert Hoover, sitting down casting in another boat. Apparently the ex-president's vision was not very good at that age and his guide had to tell him to strike when a fish came up."

That was the year the Gerstleys also fished with a then young Merl "Mac" McMullin. Gerstley:

"Later, I was fishing with Mac when I caught my largest trout up to that time. It was between 23 to 24 inches, and I still remember how excited I was and how pleased Mac was! He introduced us to the South Fork and during lunchtimes we learned much of his hunting and trapping experiences and of the riverbank vegetation and wildlife.

"One year, on a river bend just below the South Fork, we marveled at a large herd of elk crossing the river."

Except for WWII years, the Gerstleys were on the McKenzie for fishing and golf -- when not fishing abroad -- during May-June and September-October periods. In early years they did a lot of wading as well as boating.

By 1939 they were sharing their McKenzie pleasures with cousins and great friends, John and Clara Dinkelspiel of San Francisco, first in Uncle Harold's accommodations and later at Hawthorne House near Shepherd's on McKenzie Highway.

Clara Dinkelspiel remembers that summer to this day because "it was during a very hot spell." Her recollection is that host Harold Mack had "...made a killing in the bullish stock market of the Twenties ..." and " ... had retired to fish ..." while still in his thirties.

Like Cousin Jim in the beginning, neither Clara nor husband John were accomplished fly-fisherfolk. Milo Thomson also was their first guide. Clara:

"Milo placed us on a big rock, where we could fish a long run and riffle. But both Milo and his brother, Dayton, were good teachers. We stayed a long week that first trip. We also fished with Dick and Cecil Byerly at the Santiam's Detroit Reservoir area."

The following year their guides were Earl Jeans and Ed Thurston. From then on, they returned for two weeks each summer, mostly to fish with Mac McMullin, who helped them evolve into first-class anglers, both afloat and wading. Clara:

"The favorite wading places for us and for the Gerstleys were at Finn Rock ... near the Hawthorne, Edgewood, Heaven's Gate area ... and on the South Fork, under the bridge."

Once John Dinkelspiel had in turn introduced his brother and law partner, Martin, to the McKenzie, they had to alternate their vacations to keep their prominent San Francisco law firm open for business. Martin and his wife, Francis, became equally avid anglers, but not Tokatee golfers. Their son, Peter, also was bitten by the McKenzie bug.

Hawthorne House, run by Bob and Mary Porter, served the Dinkelspiels and Gerstleys most satisfactorily in those early days. Jim Gerstley:

"Their meals were huge and delicious and their flower garden a thing of beauty. Our small cabin had a shower partly outdoors. When we returned from fishing, Bob would have heated water pipes by a wood fire. Later, the Porters built the cottages at Edgewater while renovating Hawthorne House, their verandas overlooking the river."

It was on their veranda that Clara and John Diekelspiel observed follow-up circumstances to one of the river's great boating tragedies. Clara:

"We were sitting there one late afternoon when three boats in search party formation drifted by, side by side — each with a prone lookout in the bow, an oarsman, and another searcher aft. Later, we learned that Milo and two clients had drowned in a spill at Blue River."

One version was that Milo, though a veteran river runner, was so small of stature he couldn't compensate for the sudden weight shift when a very large client stood to cast and lost his balance. There was mention of alcohol being involved.

Clara also related a near miss involving another icon McKenzie guide, McMullin. At the end of their day's drift, the Dinkelspiels had stayed with Mac's boat on the south riverbank while he crossed the bridge at Finn Rock Store, to get his truck and trailer from the parking lot there. Clara:

"Just minutes before, the store's shopkeeper had been murdered in a robbery. Had Mac witnessed the get-away, he could well have been a victim too.

In the Seventies, Roger Schaad, 1998 president of our fly-club, and his wife, Sanda, were observing an anniversary at the House on the Metolius when they first met the Gerstleys. The men fished and also joined the ladies for tea on the pleasant expanse of lawn. Later, the Schaads visited the Gerstleys on the McKenzie.

The photo of Gerstley and his McKenzie steelhead was taken by Roger, who has also supplied Jim with the taking fly. In the background is the water which was a favorite wading place of Gerstley and the water the fish came from. Schaad:

"I can't now recall the pattern, and I'll bet Jim can't either. But the steelhead took it on the first drift through the run!"

BOB STEELE

McKenzie Guardian

For most of three decades, fish and game poachers along the McKenzie watershed and nearby Mohawk river valley kept a sharp lookout for one particular Oregon game warden. They breathed a collective sigh of relief when Cpl. Bob Steele retired at the close of 1971. Even toward the end of his distinguished career, Steele was wheeling his big pickup, unmarked except for mud spatters, up to 150 miles daily in his unusually effective poacher vigil. Steele had several circumstance working for him. Since 1949 he and his wife, Pat, had been property owners in the Leaburg area. Shortly, they took up residence in a home Pat designed at 17710 McKenzie Highway. They became part of the community. Even more telling, Steele held membership No. 7 in the highly regarded McKenzie River Guides Association. Members, with conservation priorities, appreciated his effectiveness. Lawful community members often were sources of information on illegal activities. But Steele's seeming omniscience also was often at work, according to Guide Dean Helfrich: "Bob always had an uncanny ability to get up in the middle of the night and get a couple of deer spotlighters. People began to believe he was unreal, and he developed an awful lot of believers!" Helfrich expressed the concern of many when he speculated, "now that Bob's retiring, probably a lot of people who haven't been poaching will start up again!"

Steele's firmness with fairness was one reason for his "always-give-a-ticket" reputation. His few detractors claimed he'd arrest anybody about anything. And Steele conceded: "you gotta be firm—and fair. But if they're in violation of a game law, then they'll be pinched, for sure." Didn't have to be a psychologist to note that while "most folks want to be checked—show you that nice mess of trout they got. It's the guy who doesn't particularly want to show you his catch that likely is a violator and gets cited." The effect that Steele had on fishermen along the McKenzie was recalled by Sgt. Zane Wilson of the Eugene police department from an incident he witnessed at age 14: "We used to fish around the rocks below Leaburg Dam and we'd watch some old boys fishing illegally. This time, they looked upriver and saw Steele rounding a curve. "Oh, god! here comes Steele, they cried. Oh, damn! What're we going to do!?!" There's no record of what they did—or Bob Steele did there and then. He did volunteer an account of a downright persistent poacher. "I caught this one guy—cited him five times in thirty minutes for snagging salmon! The last pinch was at 11 p.m. I told him he'd better quit or he was going to jail. As it was, it cost him about $150. He didn't seem mad about it, but he sure wanted those salmon!"

Steele's reputation of being everywhere was never better defined than in a story circulated along the McKenzie. A young Boy Scout was being questioned by his leader as to what procedure to follow should he be lost in the woods. The youth is said to have responded: "Well, I'd just start fishing. And then, Bob Steele would show up and find me!"

The late-July sun was still hot when I arrived at the run I wanted to fish on Oregon's lower McKenzie River. The river was lifeless in the afternoon heat. I pulled the punt to shore, pitched my small tent in the shade of a cottonwood tree and constructed an early dinner. I wouldn't want to stop fishing to eat when the water began to boil with its evening activity.

I sat at the edge of the run and ate my stew, idly watching the river, while shadows from a stand of tall trees on the other side slowly crept across the river. About the time they reached my shore, the first rise disturbed the surface. I kept on eating; one rise does not make a hatch. Soon I saw a pale yellowish mayfly dun boat the currents for a foot or two, then escape in graceful flight into the evening air.

That's when I began to bolt my stew!

—Dave Hughes
Fly-fishing Magazine
April, 1991

A River's Reincarnation

"SHE IS A NEW CARNATION OF SOME OF THE ILLUSTRIOUS DEAD."—*Jeffrey*

The mighty McKenzie today gives no hint at earlier near-death experiences of that blue ribbon trout stream. Like a cat with multiple lives, the river has managed to struggle and finally survive in grand style. As usual, Man was both the villain and the savior.

Early day log drives scoured spawning beds until that practice was halted. A major hit, however, was triggered during post WWII pesticide sprayings of much of the McKenzie watershed's nearly 1,000,000 acres. John Allen, current Forest Service District Ranger:

"Intent was to spray for epidemic populations of spruce budworm that were defoliating trees in the upper portions of the watershed."

A key savior, biologist Chris Jensen.

An important economic resource was at stake. From National Forest lands, which make up 61% of the watershed, between 750-800 million board feet were harvested from post-WWII to recent years. (Harvest figures on the 22% industrial forestlands, the 10% private use lands, the 6% BLM lands and 1% other are not accessible.) But the spraying problem was like throwing the baby out with the bath water! Longtime McKenzie guide Dave Helfrich:

"Probably the single factor that put most impact on the river was the spraying of the spruce bud beetle. They sprayed that whole high country with a strong DDT. I can remember as a kid, being up on Ennis Creek and actually seeing those little dead budworm larvae floating down the creek. Looked like food to the fish, but nearly wiped out the McKenzie fishing-wise."

For most problems, solutions sometimes emerge, and in the case of the McKenzie, it was in the form of a do-something aquatic biologist named Chris Jensen. He brought the massive fish kill to the attention of officialdom. Les Zumwalt, regional supervisor at the time:

"Biologist Jensen reported some dead fish—dead ones full of bugs—but it was not a complete kill."

Even so, something had to be done to revitalize the McKenzie fishery. " ... known from coast to coast for years as one of the finest trout streams in North America." Rainbow from Utah were introduced, but they were small fry and didn't survive very well. After several years of experimentation, legal-size trout were planted.

Jensen preparing to plant fish from a partially water filled boat while drifting downstream.

Biologist Jensen would assume an all but bigger than life role with innovative programs rebuilding healthy McKenzie trout stocks. He was the sparkplug in a five-year experimental program which included new trout planting techniques – many which he himself originated.

Most dramatic involved utilizing the maneuverability of a regular drift boat, to get the boatload of trout — attached and floating downstream ahead—into less angler-pressured waters. The old tank truck method of planting at easily accessible shoreline sites, vulnerable to eager anglers, continued. But the floating releases afforded hatchery trout more private elbowroom. McKenzie trout were getting a royal treatment from Jensen.

His greatest achievement on their behalf, however, developed a firestorm of opposition. For Oregon's 1951 angling season, Jensen proposed that all McKenzie rainbow of 14 or more inches in length must be released to protect brood stocks. His on-site studies stood him in good stead. Dick Strite, an outdoor columnist of the day, noting a catch limit of ten fish, with no more than five over 12 inches, wrote:

"Theory behind Jensen's recommendation is that catching of rainbow 14 inches or over depletes the stock of brood trout...trout that produce between 800 and 3,000 eggs annually ... for natural propagation."

Chris Jensen Jr.:

"Most, but not all, of the fishing public supported Dad's 14-inch regulation.

I remember once being with him at Paradise Campground when he had to revive a large rainbow, ready to spawn, which a person had pulled from the river and deposited in his creel!"

Protection of spawner trout worked and has been working ever since, despite initially being the most controversial angling issue of the day. In one major effort to overthrow the regulation, a charter bus full led by a prominent guide as spokesman, stormed a preliminary hearing to pressure the commission's members. Kenny King, veteran guide, in a 1977 letter to Jensen recalled:

"... pressured, the commission agreed to do so ... but two days before the final hearing ... they reversed their decision and left the regulation in effect."

King's letter reports that ultimately there was a major reversal of opposition, including that of the earlier busload's spokesman:

"He admitted to me that he had make a mistake in trying to have it removed!"

The McKenzie River Chamber of Commerce also switched from opposition to support and King, in crediting Jensen's role, wrote:

"It is definitely a conservation measure, and if you had not introduced it when you did, there would be no 'native' trout in the McKenzie today."

King's feelings revealing the intensity on both sides add an exclamation mark to his closing comment to Jensen:

"If the regulation is removed, I will 'kill' my share of 'natives' before someone else does!"

Jensen's son, Chris, Jr., remembers the early years:

"I spent a lot of time with Dad ... checking fishermen's creels ... monitoring the live fish trap at the Leaburg Dam's fish ladder ... and helping plant fish from a special boat he designed."

Young Jensen's recall of those downriver plantings are especially vivid:

"We would ride down river and plant fish ... from the special wooden boat ... a large rubber tube keeping it afloat ... despite many holes all around designed to let fresh river water circulate, providing oxygen for the fish.

"As we moved down river, we dipped fish out of that boat with a hand net. Sometimes, the fish boat would all but completely disappear in whirlpools, automatically liberating some of the fish that my Dad was trying to dip from the half submerged craft!"

Whether it was a single fish, a particular group of fish, or the entire fishery, Jensen was there on their behalf. And in bold, innovative ways, according to son Chris:

"... to get the Weyerhaeuser plant at Springfield to stop dumping their waste effluent into the McKenzie ... he set cages of live rainbow in the river below Weyerhaeuser's discharge point...killing the trout in the cages. Local press covered the story and Weyerhaeuser changed their waste disposal practices."

Jensen and his family were about to leave Eugene for Portland and a job promotion when the Eugene Water & Electric Board proposed the "Beaver Marsh Project," which would've converted the McKenzie's headwaters, Clear Lake, into a power storage reservoir. Chris, Jr. again:

"This would've resulted in the levels of Clear Lake and the McKenzie River fluctuating daily during power demands.

"As it was, after we moved to Portland, they developed the upper McKenzie for power generation. But, at least Clear Lake was saved and maintains its unique clarity still."

Biologist Jensen is remembered by a daughter, Jan Jensen of Boise, Idaho, who, although she was too young for McKenzie era memories, recognized his specialness. Jan Jensen:

"My father could always figure out how to accomplish a task with what he had. He had a creative mind, a kind heart, and a great sense of humor."

When he was promoted to chief of Oregon's fish hatcheries, memories of what he accomplished are all but legend. Not just the major projects but his little, day to day concern for every McKenzie trout's welfare.

Jurist Tongue

Excerpts from Confessions of a Fly-Fishing Judge

By Thomas H. Tongue
1919-1994

As the famous Ben Hur Lampman once wrote: "Fisherman have rediscovered the escape. The stream they fish is running through their hearts to bear away the frets and worries of yesterday and tomorrow. All fishermen know how it is, though it is uncommonly difficult to explain."

The Oregon streams that coursed through the heart of State Supreme Court Justice Tongue — all fished during his distinguished career — were many and varied, from coast line to mountain shoulder. In his Confessions, eight Oregon rivers and six Oregon creeks are named, plus seven Oregon Lakes. But have no doubt, the McKenzie was second to none as a palliative easing the pressures of Judge Tongue's early formative career challenges.

Tom Jr. and Sr.

Thanks to family and friends, Tongue already was beyond apprenticeship as a fly-fisherman when introduced by a good friend to the McKenzie's South Fork. In the summer of 1934, after graduation from the University of Oregon and law school, he enjoyed, when summer job permitted, what he described as "that idyllic summer."

His summer job in Eugene required use of an automobile. The 1927 Model T Ford he acquired for $25, did double duty in trips to the South Fork. Judge Tongue:

"The main McKenzie was difficult to fish from the bank, and was fished mostly from ... drift boats with guides.

"Not able to afford the exorbitant $10 for a guide, the next-best fishing was on its South Fork. And the best water on the South Fork was a three-mile stretch up-river from its mouth—with no road or trail for easy access.

"Whenever I could find an excuse to take an afternoon off, I would crank up the old Model T and head for the South Fork, pausing only at the old Sparks Ranch ... to ask the cook to save something for a late dinner on my way home."

From the former stagecoach stop, Tongue parked at the South Fork's mouth and "crashed ... brush" to his favorite stretch, ... where good-sized McKenzie 'redsides' could be caught on a Split Wing Caddis (before the advent of the much more serviceable and equally effective Bucktail Caddis.) Judge Tongue:

Dan Callaghan photo

Seeking a parachute pattern.

"I would fish until dusk, then crawl out of the river, waderless and soaking wet, and head for Sparks Ranch where excellent food was served 'family style' on platters and in large bowls."

Surviving the first and most grueling law school year, he worked as compass-man for a logging company's timber cruiser. Earning enough to replace the '27 Model T he'd had to sell, Tongue updated his transportation, for $65, with a used 1928 Model A Ford. Judge Tongue:

"It still had a crank for use when the 'starter' would not work." Its gasoline tank was under the hood with a 'cap' in front of the windshield, and it had a 'rumble seat'. With these new 'wheels' I was again able to enjoy the South Fork!

In his Confessions, Tongue's South Fork memories are many and memorable. Tongue:

"... asked by a friend to take with me a freshman being 'rushed' by my fraternity and who professed to be a skilled fly-fisherman ... I took the 'rushee' to a likely stretch of water and then went downstream to fish. Soon I was aroused by frantic shouts to 'bring your net!' I found the freshman standing on a large rock at a deep pool's edge, his rod bent almost double, beseeching me to wade in and 'net the monster!'

"Not wishing to offend this prospective fraternity 'rushee.' I bravely waded in up to my 'belly button' to the point where his tugging line entered the water. I had not yet seen the 'monster,' but then it surfaced to my net— an 18-inch whitefish with a mouth like a sucker!

"I still can't understand why my fraternity pledged that 'fly fisherman!' "

On an early spring trip to the South Fork, Tongue learned a hard lesson when he "... undertook to wade across the river at a place where I had crossed many times before. I did not remember that those occasions were in the summer and fall, when the water was low.

"Suddenly, about half-way across—at the point of no return—gravel started to wash out from under my feet, and I found myself floating down the river!"

Judge Tongue, though heavy boots and clothing made it difficult to keep his nose above water, was not then frightened but was focused on solving his predicament. The solution, downstream, was a log extending out into the current. Tongue:

"... it was all I could do to swim that ten yards across current to that log. Only then ... did I become frightened upon realization of my close call ... a good lesson in wading for future reference. But, at the cost of Father's Hardy rod and reel!"

An incident Judge Tongue declared "one of my most memorable visits to the South Fork was during World War II, after I had been rejected from service as a 30-year-old with bad eyes."

He located a friend with sufficient coupons for then-rationed gasoline to drive to the South Fork. Judge Tongue:

"With few fishermen on the river at that time, we had a ball! We fished until dark and only then realized we must find lodging for the night. Only open place was old Belknap Springs Lodge, where the dining room was closed for the night."

The lodge, however, had a meager selection of groceries for sale to campers. All meats and butter were rationed, and Tom and companion were able to purchase a loaf of bread, apple butter and potato chips. Judge Tongue:

"Fortunately, my friend brought along a bottle of Southern Comfort, one of the few whiskeys available due to war-time rationing. (As anyone who has experienced Southern Comfort will well remember—it need not have been rationed to find few who would purchase it, given any choice in the matter.

"So my friend and I went to our small room, sat on the edge of our beds, spread slices of bread with apple butter and, after a swig of Southern Comfort, would say—upon handing a slice to one another— 'Have another slice of prime roast beef!'"

As soon as Judge Tongue felt he could now afford a guide—then $100 for a party of two—he returned to the McKenzie. Judge Tongue:

"... to float that most beautiful river in a guided drift boat."

Of Judge Crawford, Tongue added:

"Judge Crawford also had quite a sense of humor. He once took a bad fall on one knee in wading the McKenzie. On return to Cedarwood Lodge, he was asked by a California tourist how he hurt his knee. The Judge replied, 'a fish bit it!' The tourist, quite surprised, then asked, 'what kind of a fish would do that?'

"To which the Judge replied, 'a damn mean fish!'"

Gradually, through experience, Judge Tongue developed a preference for just two McKenzie guides. Judge Tongue:

"One of my two favorite guides on the McKenzie was Frank Brown. Frank was the only guide that I knew who would skin trout before frying them for a lunch stop.

(As reported elsewhere, other McKenzie guides also skinned their lunch fish.)

Once Brown's procedure had been followed, it was like "... taking a glove off one's hand. According to Frank, this could only be done with fresh-caught small trout, eight to ten inches in length."

Food often was a conversation topic, so Judge Tongue was reporting to Brown his experiences in England, including lunch in London at "the" fly-fishers club. Before the main course of poached salmon he was urged to try the appetizer, hard-boiled eggs. Dipped in the club's special sauce, they were most delicious. Judge Tongue:

"I was then told they were seagull eggs! To which Brown exclaimed, 'how could you eat the egg of a seagull, which feeds on carrion!?! My replay was to ask Frank how he liked Oregon's widely acclaimed Dungeness crab?"

Brown eventually shared with Tongue another guide's "trick," virtually painless removal of fly hook barbs imbedded in various parts of one's anatomy. Judge Tongue:

"Since then, by this method, I have removed fly hooks from friends, and have had two removed from me by friends."

Brown would leave the McKenzie August 1st to guide out of Lucas Lodge on the Rogue River, where his clients used floating lines and sub-surface flies developed by Frank. Judge Tongue:

"One good morning and evening, my English friend and I caught and mostly released twenty-five 'half-pounders," including some doubles on the dropper fly.

"Around the supper table that night, fishermen and their guides would try to get Frank to reveal the identity of that especially effective fly. Frank enjoyed all this hugely, but would never tell his secret.

"As the ultimate measure of his secrecy, Frank would clip the flies from the leaders on the rods of his fishermen just before returning to the boat landing, where other guides might otherwise see them."

"My other and all-time favorite guide is Merl (Mac) McMullin—'Mr. Mckenzie'."

As the McMullin/Tongue relationship grew, they began to trade tall fish stories. Mac struck first—about steelhead jumping into his boat—and wound up with a snake-eating trout yarn. Judge Tongue:

"Mac swears that when cleaning a ten-inch fish, he found a snake inside, folded up like an accordion, and twelve inches in length!

"When I next fished with Mac the following year, I told him I could top his fish/snake story. I had been to a place where I had fish eating from my hands and had also seen fish jumping two feet out of the water to nip bugs

Tom Tongue with guide Frank Brown.

on overhanging branches.

"While Mac was mulling this over, I confessed that the hand-feeding occurred during a cruise ship stop at one of the Virgin Islands, where tropical fish at a coral reef would take food pellets from one's hand...

"...and that I had seen a television account of good-sized fish on the upper Amazon River waiting for their favorite food — a species of beetle — to fall from leafy branches overhanging the water. Occasionally one would jump as high as two feet out of the water to get a beetle."

There is no record of whether this believe-it-or-not competition continued.

In his time, Judge Tongue was, in several ways, an ambassador of good will between Oregon and the British Islands. The only highlight of fishing at Arundel Arms in Devon was to meet Scotsman Robert Leith-Macgregor. Judge Tongue:

"In the course of our conversation I showed him some of my parachute-tied dry flies, which he had never seen. I then gave him two 'Floating Fools,' a parachute pattern developed by my friend Dale LaFollette..."

The next season, Leith-Macgregor, as a last resort, used one of those Floating Fools, when all English patterns to rising trout on one of his favorite rivers had failed. Judge Tongue:

"He said the trout came under that fly as if to say they had never seen anything like it, but then could not resist it and took the fly!

Still later, he reported a London shop duplicated the pattern for him, which he named the "Wee Macgregor. He enclosed a news clipping from an unidentified source stating the fly had been the best fly of the season on that river!

Fly-fishing was a family tradition, though at age six in 1918, Tom Tongue was initiated into angling in popular boyhood fashion—a bamboo pole, string line, large hook with worm attached. When he yanked a six-inch Gales Creek rainbow into bushes behind, he ran to the family's tent camp. Judge Tongue:

"... my father, after praising my accomplishment, told me of a somewhat similar experience when he was my age, in about 1885, when his family was then camped on the Wilson River. The annual three-day journey by horse-drawn wagons was from Hillsboro for two weeks of camping at Netarts near Tillamook. His dad praised his first trout, but then asked about his fishing rod, left behind in the excitement.

"On next year's trip my father allowed me to go with him while he fished for an afternoon on Gales Creek.. I was not allowed a rod of my own, but followed him up the creek as he cast his fly."

Two years passed before Uncle Burke built a beach home at Pacific City on the Nestucca River, changing the Tongue's fishing focus. Judge Tongue:

"On about the third summer vacation at Pacific City, father came down with my Uncle Burke and another uncle who professed an interest in finding a stream where he could fish with fly."

The upper Nestucca was chosen and young Tom and a cousin were allowed to go along. Judge Tongue:

"... we were each given one fly to cast to keep us busy and happy while the men fished ... my first experience in fishing with a fly! Small trout struck too quickly to be hooked. Then, while standing on a log bridge, my pleasure was short-lived when I snapped off my only fly on an ill-timed back-cast.

"Next summer, when I was twelve years old, Father bought a small log cabin on Scoggins Creek ... it was heaven for a boy just learning to fish with a fly! Father provided an old split-bamboo rod, some gut leaders and a few dry flies. At Honeyman Hardware store in Portland, well-tied dry flies sold for fifteen cents. Four of the happiest summers of my life were spent at our cabin on Scoggins Creek!"

At sixteen, summer jobs took priority and Tom's father insisted he work out-of-doors ... on a farm ... with a survey crew ... or in a logging camp. Result: he became even more devoted to streams and their settings. Judge Tongue:

"For first years of my retirement ... I had the great pleasure of introducing my grandson, another Tom, to the pleasures of fly-fishing. My other grandson, Christopher, was born too late for me to be able to do such things with him."

But Tongue could take satisfaction in knowing he had perpetuated the family's fly-fishing interests. Sons Tom, John and Jim and were streamside with him at an early age, as was Grandaughter Kathryn. Lisa and Laura were born too late to join in the family's small outings.

As an octogenarian with impaired lungs, "Grandpa's" thoughts often turned to how it all would end. He recalled the fate of a good friend, a Eugene attorney who retired at 80 to a small farm and a drift boat on the lower McKenzie River. Judge Tongue:

"He loved that river! He went fishing with a good friend a few miles above his place, where he planned to take out. Toward the end of an almost futile day, he tied on an old, bushy bucktail caddis he had dressed himself.

"Almost immediately, and not far above his home landing place, he hooked and landed a sixteen-inch McKenzie redside—then suffered a stroke and fell over dead in his boat.

"What a way to go! Would that I or any other true fly-fisherman could be so fortunate!"

A McKENZIE MYSTERY

How could a 1953 Eugene High School graduate, who had honed his fly-fishing skills on McKenzie watershed, completely ignore his home river in his wildly successful "Trout Fishing in America?" The answer may lie with a schoolmate and close friend who was, in fact even more than a special fishing chum of the late Richard Brautigan.

"When I wouldn't loan Richard $5 until he cleared up an accumulated debt totaling $20, he left our house in a rage," the Rev. Peter Webster recalls. "He vented that anger by throwing a rock through a jailhouse window, was arrested and evaluated and sent to Salem for extensive electro-shock therapy. No doubt he left some of his memory there."

In his slim 112-page book, Brautigan writes of 73 rivers, creeks, lakes and hot springs in the Sixties and Seventies eras – but not a single McKenzie mention. In fact, "Trout Fishing"... was begun beside an Idaho stream, when Brautigan would set his old portable typewriter on a rickety campsite card table.

Yet he and Webster and Stanley Oswald had many McKenzie experiences vividly recalled by Webster:

"Richard was the purist of our group – almost. He didn't carry a creel for nothing. At rare times he might use a salmon egg. I was the night crawler user. However, Richard would help harvest the worms and share in the resulting profits."

Catch-and-release wasn't as big in Brautigan's youth as it apparently became later at his Montana ranch. Keith Abbott in his "Downstream From Trout Fishing in America", a Memoir of Richard Brautigan, reports:

"Only fishing for sport himself, Richard usually released any trout he caught, and hardly ever kept them for eating. If he did, he made sure they were young and pan size, ten inches long at most."

❧❧❧

The young Eugene threesome, always scrounging for spending money, collected, 1,500 night crawlers by flashlight one evening, visiting residential lawns and the University of Oregon campus. Webster:

"We sold them for a penny apiece at the grocery store at Cedar Flats, just upriver out of Springfield. The store then sold them to fisherman for 25 cents a dozen.

"That was, it turned out, our biggest financial deal – better than selling Christmas Trees."

Brautigan endured a miserable, lonely childhood wherein angling was one of his rare pleasures. In "Trout Fishing In America" he wrote:

"As a child when did I first hear about trout fishing in America? From whom? I guess it was a stepfather of mine. Summer of 1942. The old drunk told me about trout fishing. When he could talk..."

The Websters became Brautigan's exofficio family and were so honored later, after a book published in Mrs. Webster's name came out. Both mother and son were at the book signing of Edna Webster's "Undisclosed Manuscripts of Richard Brautigan" in the hippie generation's popular bookstore in San Francisco's Haight-Ashbury district.

For their mostly McKenzie fishing trips, Webster provided the wheels and Brautigan the experience and tackle. Webster:

"Our first trip together, up the McKenzie's South Fork, was in my 1937 four-door Ford, painted green with house paint and with brush marks plainly evident to prove it. Richard and Stan got 23 fish while I got experience, untangling leader and line knots."

Fishing became their mutual passion. By working night shift at Eugene Fruit Growers plant, they managed to chase McKenzie trout during some daylight hours. Webster:

"We hiked and fished upstream to Clear Lake, rented a boat there and fished the lake. And we liked little, cascading Indian Creek where the trout were very small but the scenery was marvelous! Gate Creek was a downstream challenge."

Only youthful nimbleness spared the waders from serious spill as they literally skated over rocky shallows in cheap tennis shoes with no socks. Webster wasn't so lucky in the swift waters surrounding an island at Armitage Park:

"I had a can of worms in one hand, my creel over my back, and my rod in the other. Got thoroughly doused in the crossing, only to learn my worms had washed out of the can. I went home."

Webster recollects that Brautigan's McKenzie favorite was the Blue River area, although he took his biggest fish—a 13 inch redside—on a fly at Gate Creek. Webster:

"When I knew Richard he was a tall, skinny drink of water—six-foot-three and only 163 pounds. He never, ever learned to drive and sometimes hitchhiked up to fifty miles just to go fishing."

The Brautigan/Webster relationship continued to bloom after their 1953 high school graduation, when Peter became a freshman at Northwest Christian College. Brautigan would read his from his latest efforts while Webster worked on term papers. Webster:

"It was, as much as anything, Richard's unusual voice that made his reading of his poems and other works so fascinating to me. When he went on to California and his big yet brief moment of fame, he asked me to come with him. But I was committed to becoming a minister."

Webster bought that old Ford when he was 19 and before he had learned to drive, his learner's permit requiring a licensed driver accompany him. His first upgrade was to a 1946 DeSoto.

Just down river from Goodpasture Island was a whitefish fishery where they sometimes enjoyed catch-and-release action with flies. No keepers: they had the bland consistency of wet soda crackers. Below Leaburg Dam Richard and Peter watched for an hour an angler playing a 25-pound salmon

By working the night shift at the cannery, they managed to chase trout during some of their remaining daylight hours. One opening day they hit a bonanza near an outfall pipe under the highway at Leaburg Lake. Webster later, working at the Huntington Shingle Mill in Springfield, got chances to fish upriver from work's end at 3:30 until sunset. He remained, basically, a worm and salmon egg fisherman. Once, lacking either, he caught a lively grasshopper and, caught a fine trout.

Their paths parted in 1954. In 1969, Reverend Webster was looking in one of Brautigan's several books, which listed his phone number. He called the number from Hoquiam, then his pastorate, and Brautigan answered. Webster:

"We resumed our conversation just as if there hadn't been a 15-year lapse! McKenzie trout fishing memories were exchanged!"

In mid-2000, Webster ended his 44-year ministerial career—which had begun, interestingly, on the banks of the McKenzie. His first student at church had been at Waltersville, between Cedar Flat and Leaburg.

That idyllic period at Waltersville was Webster's last serious fishing effort. Ever a wader then, and only once a rubber rafter, he still has his own flight of fancy regarding the McKenzie:

"It's my dream to take a drift boat trip down that river just once, regardless of the cost!"

Brautigan, whose flights of fancy were required reading for the hip generation – when "Trout Fishing in America" sold two million copies throughout the world and it and other writings were translated into seventeen languages—would approve.

The Francis Generations

Name a landmark challenge in McKenzie River Valley and Win Francis, Bend attorney, has been there and done that! A fourth generation Francis fly-fisherman (his son, Kirby, and daughter, Teal, make it five!) finally settled on the McKenzie as his main love after sampling other great northwest/Canadian waters.

Buddies Eddie Miller (left) and Win Francis ward off opening day chills.

Ask him what he has done—other than drift boating from upriver Olallie to confluence with the Willamette—and he will recite an eclectic list of adventures which set him apart as a special outdoorsman. Not surprising because the exploration urge was in the blood of his father, C. Ed Francis, and his grandfather, Clarence E. Francis, as well as that of his great-grandfather, Clarence Almeron.

Win wasn't yet a teen-ager when Prince Helfrich took him under his wing. At first he was a paying client. Then later, from grade school through college, he earned his keep as a baggage boatman. In those days, Prince

Grandfather Clarence Francis relaxing before lunch on a 1938 drift.

would build a new boat every winter. Francis:

"It was always a big issue with us young boatmen to see who got to row that new boat, be it on McKenzie, John Day or Rogue trips."

There was one opening day he especially remembers:

"Three of us high school kids camped out in a two-man tent. It rained, and even the comfort of some whiskey we had filched from family sources didn't soften the misery. I was between my buddies. Each time I put my head down there was a splash! We gave up and moved to the car!"

They also were part of the problem which led to demise of the traditional and colorful McKenzie boat parade. Francis:

"We created great rafts out of inner tubes ... the most exciting parade I recall was in my falling off our raft at the head of Martin's Rapid. I was not wearing a life jacket!"

Both Francis and his companion, still on their raft, survived. Francis again:

"At the rapid's end, my friend asked me to swim out a retrieve a can of beer which had washed from his grasp during the ordeal!"

While beginning his law practice in Bend, young Francis acquired a retreat near McKenzie Bridge yet still handy to his eastern Oregon base. From that retreat, he has hiked or biked the entire McKenzie River Trail from Fish Lake to that bridge.

From there also, Francis created many adventuresome memories ... a climb of Eagle Rock—in waders—on a rainy day ... pointedly running every possible side channel the spring McKenzie offered. Francis:

"Many the time my river floating partner, Eddy Miller, and I had to go over the side to haul our boat over a shallow spot or around a log-blocked channel."

For years, beginning in the Seventies, transport for his rivers experiences was in a classic drift boat built by the pioneering Woodie Hindman but owned by a LaPine, OR outdoorsman. Francis:

"He had the most meticulous garage I had ever seen! We were instantly assured he would be the right guy to buy a drift boat from. And it was, by far, the nicest rowing boat I ever owned."

Francis also had a long, wide-bottomed, high-sided Clackacraft which he thought was going to last him forever. Francis:

"However, two friends borrowed it for a high-water float on the Deschutes in March. Coming through Buckskin Mary, so they told me, a wave flipped them backwards. While they struggled to shore, my boat drifted, overturned and submerged. In the next rapid, it was pinned upon a large rock and broke up on the bottom."

The replacement boat will be a tin one, Win explaining that as much as I'd have liked to stay with wooden boats, times change and a tin boat is more easily maintained."

One recent Francis family outing involved a small rubber raft, upended in the McKenzie just to build confidence that the occupants would be prepared to handle such emergencies.

A favorite memory, was created when Win personally took his Dad in his drift boat down the Salmon's Middle Fork. To assure a pleasant trip of ultra comfort, Win had hoped for one of Prince's sons to do the camp and cooking chores. The second generation Helfrich's were busy but, at the agreed-upon rendezvous on the river, a young fellow introduced himself as Jeff, a third generation Helfrich! Francis:

"I was stunned, I had fished with and worked for his grandfather!"

Marcile Cowlin

By any measure, Marcile Cowlin's love affair with the McKenzie River has been singular and extraordinary, thriving more than fifty trout seasons. At each summer's end, she and her seventh McKenzie guide, Wade Thomas, indulge in some not-so-small talk along these lines: Marcile, 99, concludes her "goodbye" with a comment that it probably has been her last trip.

Wade counters, "Don't be ridiculous! I'll see you next year!"

And he has.

Wade talked with Marcile in May 2000, when she was getting ready to go to her favorite gambling casino for her usual two days of playing 21. When he said he expected to see her on the end of a rod this summer, Marcile said she was "old," feeling "old," being "old."

During Marcile's five-boat family float in 1999 Wade said she fished all day, although she wasn't feeling very well, and was furious when it was time to call it a day. Family members fished, shared in a huge fish fry at lunchtime. Balance of "keeper" catch was taken to Holiday Farm, where it is assumed the fish were frozen and taken to Portland. Wade said Marcile got a bit cranky ... perhaps because it was really hot and she wasn't feeling at her best.

"I've always been a purist," she vows. "I've never used worms."

She was taught to fish by a teen-age sweetheart, Tom Malarkey, at a trout farm near Gearhart.

"I'd die if I couldn't fish this river," she once exclaimed.

Of luncheon fish fries— "The tail is one of the best parts ... It tastes just like bacon."

During that half-century, she has watched guiding fees go from $15 for a day on the river to $220.

Of increasing river traffic-- especially the rafters who yell, drink beer, and soak one another with water buckets and squirt guns, she says it doesn't affect her fishing .... "No, just my disposition."

Of the suggestion that someone bring her fish when she no longer can catch them herself .... "It's not the fish. It's the fishing."

Even so, the Cowlin party almost always takes home limits of "keepers." And family trips generally began with a bet for the first fish caught ... and for the biggest.

The late Dr. Ernest Livingstone, son-in-law, once dismissed her comment, she wouldn't make it back another year with:

"Every year has been her 'last year' for the last three years!"

THE PETERSENS

Baltzer Petersen's concept of fishing and that of his trout-focused bride, Louise, were "poles apart," you might say, but their eventual many years on the McKenzie proved that a good, strong marriage can survive anything!

Their Canadian honeymoon provided the acid test. At their destination, the bride began unpacking her fly-fishing gear. Trout in her family's New Jersey property pond had imprinted her at an early age. She was ecstatic, the bridegroom was hysterical. They were going out for salmon, not fly fishing, he informed her. It was a learning experience she remembers:

"My husband was in the salmon canning business in Alaska, and he took a dim view of fly-fishing!"

The Petersens had been McKenzie visitors long before acquiring their riverbank place on McKenzie River Drive in 1965. Though it was never given a name, as were some along the river, it became well known for fishing and dinner parties for adults and for children during the several decades that followed. And each time the Petersens closed it for the winter, Louise would part with:

"I just can't wait to get back to my beloved McKenzie!"

Nor did she ever lose that same sort of affection for the place of her fishy beginnings. When trout in her family's pond faced starvation several years ago, she hired a helicopter to drop feed for the fish.

On the McKenzie, she was proud of her big collection of certificates honoring her release of spawner-size native rainbow, yet at the same time had no qualms about harvesting planter trout for current and future meals. In fact, the freezer at Phil's Phine Pfood's, about a mile downriver, became secondary storage for Louise's fish in milk cartons. At summer's end, they were carefully transported to California for winter meals.

Virtually all of her Rainbow Club release certificates had been signed by her favorite guide, Ennis Nestle, in the Seventies.

There were two unique conveniences for Louise at the Petersen's summer place. First, there was remarkably easy access to the river so that she could wade out from the deck area and fish, yet keep an eye on her mother and her husband as the years took their toll on their health. Then, Harold Carlson, a local contractor, had fashioned for her out of an enormous hollow cedar stump what became her handy fishing tackle closet. Carlson crafted a large bark door with wooden handle and big wooden pegs inside for hanging waders and other gear. (The next owner of the property did away with the charming landmark.)

Granddaughters of lifelong flyfisherman Louise Petersen loved to pose here enroute to Grandma "Weezie's" summer place on the McKenzie.

Louise Petersen's fishing focus was such that she could ignore pain and hardships. Once when instructing grandchildren on how to cast and fish she hooked her thumb with her fly. She calmly cut the leader, tied on a new fly and continued to fish and instruct.

And her sense of humor was quite healthy as well. During the frequent McKenzie visits, granddaughters would be picked up at the Eugene airport. Returning to the river along Airport Road there always was a required photo op at the sign reading, LONG'S LONGLIFE WORMERY. A longtime McKenzie neighbor and friend, Tuck Thomas, remembers:

"Louise thought this hysterically funny, probably because she never used worms and couldn't care less whether or not they enjoyed a long life!"

What she did care about was the health of her special river. Invariably she would end her notes from her California base with a ringing slogan-like exclamation:

"SAVE MY MCKENZIE!"

A Wader by Choice

Theodore L. Keusseff
1905—1996

After thousands of hours of wading "tit deep" in McKenzie currents, rock-solid Ted Keusseff finally eased up on fishing local waters. But not on wading! He had discovered steelhead in the Dean River.

In a 1990 interview at his longtime riverbank home near Blue River, Ted admitted: "I don't fish this (McKenzie) river anymore, damnit! There was a time when, in some years, I caught thirty steelhead here. That spoiled me, and when the numbers dropped dramatically, I began going up to the Dean. This year will be my 24th year up there!"

Ted had already paid his deposit for 1996 season wading rights on the Dean. That Dean trip deposit was refunded after he died following a stroke in late April of that year. He had long ago "paid his dues" to his last home river. Though a bank fisherman since Utah boyhood, Keusseff recognized he needed the local expertise offered by McKenzie guides and signed up for several drift boat trips.

Bob Welch photo

Keusseff and Mac McMullin looking over 10th Anniversary Creel.

"They were the best," he remembered—"John West, Prince and his Helfrich brood, and Merl "Mac" McMullin. I learned a lot from them about the McKenzie."

Once he had noted, from drift boat vantage points, the likely fishy places, Keusseff returned to wading. Several McKenzie "catch" memories stuck in Ted's mind. At Brooks Riffle, numerous blackbirds were competing with Ted for the "McKenzie Specials"—big green drakes hatching from deep water. Ted finally leader-lassoed one blackbird flying behind him. An unusual diversion! He also remembered:

"In the Seventies, I used to catch 'Old Joe' in the foamy spillover just below Trailbridge Dam, an afterdam for salmon enhancement. Old Joe was a heavy rainbow of about eighteen inches, and I caught him five or six times that I know of. He must've liked it!"

After several close calls on the Deschutes and Salmon rivers, Ted decided he was too old to comfortably become a whitewater man. But, not too old to begin his quest, at age seventy, for the coveted Grand Slam of rams! His last of seven sheep—a Mongolian Argali taken at 12,000-plus feet elevation, at age eighty—overqualified him for that Grand Slam, awarded in 1988.

❧❧❧

Lee Richardson, another remarkable vintage sportsman remembered elsewhere in this journal, called Ted's idyllic home retreat his "favorite resting pond." If one chose, he could stand at edge of the imposing stone veranda, a stiff Scotch (86 proof Bulloch & Lades) in one hand and cast comfortably upon waters of the northern branch of the McKenzie.

Ted's ashes are scattered at Lee's "favorite resting pond." His classic tackle, however, still meets trout and steelhead challenges of the McKenzie and Willamette rivers, thanks to a sensitive collector and wader, Daniel L. Brock. He had acquired Keusseff's considerable and special tackle inventory, including E. C. Powell bamboo rods and steelhead and trout reels built by Ted along Hardy Perfect lines.

Brock lives near Big Falls Creek, near junction of the Willamette and McKenzie rivers. He can be fishing the "Willy" in five minutes and wading the McKenzie in twenty minutes. And he does, when the mood strikes him. It struck him recently when he acquired and read, non-stop, "Tommy Brayshaw, The Ardent Angler-Artist". Brock:

"I was again inspired to go to my rod closet, take out Keusseff's nine-foot Powell steelhead rod and head for the 'Willy'. The idea was to enjoy the day with a fine rod, reflecting upon the book I had just devoured.

"At second cast, there was a solid grab and a terrific run. My reel jammed, the steelhead jumped and it was all over! What a great interruption of my afternoon's reflections.

"Crossing the pool to the far bank, I resumed casting. Again, at second cast, there was a twitch and a grab as my fly swung below me.

"Several jumps and runs later, I tailed and released a beautiful hen of about twelve pounds—a robust fish destined to remain in one's memories. As she swam away I rubbed some of her slime on that old Powell, for it had come full circle once again.

"I waded back to the other side, sat on the bank, letting the wonder of it all sink in. Then I waded out knee-deep and started casting again as if to prolong the experience.

"A third fish! Another hen of about seven pounds—contributed to the magic of the moment! Quickly fought, landed, and released, she completed a dream day.

DAN CALLAGHAN

Dan Callaghan's long-standing love affair with moving water is only hinted at in his classic McKenzie Creel cover photo. He is globally known as without peer among anglers who also take river pictures. It is no coincidence that his auto license plates spells OUZEL, tribute to one of his favorite watery way companions.

Fly-fishing came first, ahead of photography, in Dan's youth. His second goal when launching a career as a corporate lawyer at Willamette University, Salem, was to learn to fly fish. The McKenzie River was nearby, and Callaghan fortuitously contacted Prince Helfrich, celebrated river guide. He remembers: "Of course, going to school, I couldn't afford much fishing. I asked Prince how much a half-day would cost. There was a pause. I remember that. And then he said "five dollars!"

"I didn't know how to fly fish at all! I think I had one or two flies and an old fly rod. Prince was very, very nice to me, showing me a lot about casting. I think I even caught some fish! That half-day went by so fast I couldn't believe it!"

Dan fished a few more times with Prince, then his sons, and another McKenzie guide, Wayne Loder, who, like Prince, no longer lives. It wasn't too long, however, before his romance with the North Umpqua began. The attraction there, at Steamboat Inn, was the then-proprietor, Frank Moore, who in Dan's estimation still is the Arnold Palmer of the North Umpqua. Dan recalls: "I was camping out on my first Umpqua trip, met Frank and asked, did he take people out. "Depends on if you're staying here," he said. "How much?" I asked.

"Five dollars a night ... dinner is extra." "How much?" I again asked. "Two dollars," he said, "except when we have steak. Then it's two-and-a-quarter!"

"Frank was a good teacher and, if he liked you, he'd pause in his heavy workload at Steamboat to take you fishing. He isn't a big man, but still incredibly fit, and has timing that makes a long double-haul look easy. I had a lot more to learn, and he enjoyed showing me how to do it right!"

Callaghan was fishing the Umpqua when he met Jack Hemingway at Steamboat, just after Jack's father, Ernest, checked out.

"We got to be very good friends and fished over one hundred rivers together," Dan recalls. "My wife, Mary Kay, and I are godparents to one of his daughters. And when Jack was married a second time, I was his best man.

"There was a big garden ceremony in Ketchum, Idaho, and when I was supposed to give him the ring, I instead pulled from my tux pocket a Hemingway Caddis! You should've seen the expression on his face! After he took it and put it in his lapel, I gave him the ring."

The close personal relationship continued under an arrangement called Hemingway & Callaghan Enterprises, which wasn't always that enterprising, until Jack's death. Callaghan: "We had an idea for a book on the 100th anniversary of his father's life to be called Papa's Paris. I did photographs of old Hemingway haunts in Paris, but Jack never did finish the text.

Beginning with Brownie cameras as a young boy, then graduating to a Kodak Retina in the mid-Fifties, Callaghan had no clue to an upcoming upgrade in his priorities. Dan: "I really got passionate about photography looking at Ralph Wahl's black-and-white pictures at the first FFF conclave in Eugene in 1965. Got my first Nikon and slowly began including black-and-white in my shooting priorities. Ralph taught me his system and how to frame. Eventually, Flyfisher magazine was using a lot of my stuff."

Increasingly, fly-fishing and photography competed for his time as a lawyer In fact, his major account, Umpqua Feather Merchants, accounted for 40% of his corporate business at time of his retirement. Now, he has more time to sit down with a book from his extensive fly fishing library, and to dress a few flies.

Dan's personal calling card lists Cabin One (his home-away-from home at Steamboat Inn) and a water ouzel about to execute the characteristic dipper action. His memories of being on a stream with the unique bird some call the "teeter-ass" are mostly very pleasant.

However, he becomes somber when recalling how a road crew widening McKenzie River highway wiped out the nest of a family of ouzels at the junction of a feeder stream and the main river.

"They were like family," he remembers.

Listing of John Daniel Callaghan's considerable achievements isn't possible here. Highlights include his five-year term as a commissioner on what is now known as the state's Fish and Wildlife Commission. Oregon and the McKenzie in particular are the better for his environmental work.

He was instrumental in helping found several conservation-oriented organizations and currently is a member and supporter of several dozen such groups in the west. Notably, he also was house counsel and board member for the FFF for 15 years, a director of The Museum of American Fly fishing, and recipient, in 1985, of Oregon Trout's "Wild Trout Award."

Dan has fly-fished and photographed in most western states, Canada, and Alaska, as well as Europe, Iceland, Central and South America. Beyond contributing to fly fishing periodicals, his photographs have appeared in Newsweek, Country Gentlemen, etc. When he completes his part of re-publication of the 1938 classic, Howard Back's "The Waters of the Yellowstone with Rod and Fly," Callaghan's photographs will have been featured in a half-dozen books.

The McKenzie River Creel is what it is in large measure because of Dan Callaghan.

Refloat!

By Spencer Erhman

If one word can epitomize and define a fly-fishing experience on a river, and if one word can be used to paint a picture of that same river, then the word for Oregon's McKenzie River is—REFLOAT![1]

In the sixty-eight years since I first fished this beautiful river, 538,650 people also have fished it—give or take a few. Some were self-propelled, but most were with one of the many expert guides. Individually and collectively, they have talked themselves hoarse, telling their dudes where and how to fish. And becoming more callous-handed rowing their drift boats until the dudes finally caught on. And what was the magic word that all those guides have repeated through the years? You got it—REFLOAT!

Guide Dayton Thomson said it to me first some time in the summer of 1933 on my first trip down the river with my late father, Mason Ehrman. Dayton was a quiet man and father's favorite boatman. Dad was an excellent fisherman and needed neither help or advice on where to cast his flies or what to do with them, once cast. He and Dayton could fish all day together with not more than ten words exchanged between them.

But not so with his young and exuberant son, me, who had been taught the rudiments of casting a fly on the lawn of his parents' home. Having the need to show off his new found skill to transfer a fly from the air to the water, I would immediately pick it up and cast it again. And again, and again, and again. Mister Thomson (I was brought up to call all male adults "mister") finally said something to me—something very basic and very important:

"You can't catch fish if your fly isn't on the water!"

And then, after my very next cast, I heard the magic word for the very first time: "REFLOAT!" Followed by an explanation of all that that word meant!

Fishing was outstanding in those early days, especially the hooking, the playing, and the landing. The limit was twenty fish and, unfortunately, it did not occur to many anglers to release the bulk of their catch. It was not difficult to catch and keep a limit of rainbows averaging more than fifteen inches long. Results of that lack of foresight linger today.

My parents used to spend several weekends every fishing season at Thomson's Lodge near Vida. It was a mecca for McKenzie River fly-fishermen, the lodging and meals being as excellent as the guiding and fishing. As I recall, the price for all-day fishing with a guide was $8, and that included a very large lunch!

Carey Thomson (1897-1940) was joined in guiding by three sons—Dayton, Milo, and York. His wife, Elvira, and those of the sons, all contributed to the great ambiance of their lodge. I don't recall the capacity, but the lodge always seemed full when we were there. Getting to the lodge, however, presented one final hurdle for the faint-hearted.

Situated on the river's south bank, guests had to park their autos on the north bank and navigate a narrow, swaying suspension foot bridge I recall that my mother would not set foot on it, so she was always transported by "water taxi"—a McKenzie drift boat. I, too, did not look favorably on setting foot on that bridge, but my pride would not let me join my mother, so I walked that bridge ... slowly ... and carefully.

One trip I shall never forget. My boatman was Everett Spaulding, an accomplished guide. This day, everyone from Thomson's Lodge headed upriver to fish. When I suggested to Everett that we go downstream, he argued strenuously against it as follows:

"... river's too low ... you'll be with me, pushing the boat over rocks ... too much work!"

From left: Author Ehrman, Win Francis, late Ed Francis, Dr. Len Dick.

Maybe a case of the customer always being right, because downstream we went after our put in below Leaburg Dam. That low water stretch required we get out a few times to boost the boat through the shallows. But the extra effort was worth it!

Salmon there were at height of their spawning, and rainbows were feasting on eggs drifting out of spawning redds. By just casting over the spawning beds, I had my best day's fishing ever on the river, Everett reminding me occasionally to REFLOAT.

What capped that sensational day was that when we returned to the lodge, none of the upstream anglers had enjoyed our success. Ours was the only boat to catch fish! Everett was as happy as I was!

Another guide I remember very fondly was George Leslie. He guided my sister, Alayne, and me several times after World War II, and we always caught fish. REFLOATING helped a lot!

For the last dozen or so years we have opened the McKenzie trout season with Len Dick, the late Ed Francis, and the late Charlie Miller and our sons. (Spencer Dick, Win Francis, Eddie Miller, and Spencer, Jr.) Fishing is seldom great, but the camaraderie and the REFLOATING are terrific. We stayed at the Wayfarer Lodge, across the covered Goodpasture Bridge, and did our own cooking, which is surprisingly excellent. Helene Dick always sends a rhubarb pie, which is wonderful and doesn't need REFLOATING.

Guides Ken Helfrich and Gary Williams have been my guides in most recent years, followed by Al Plath; all, of course, accomplished devotees of the art of REFLOATING.

In the mid-Eighties, Ken Helfrich talked us into what turned out to be an unforgettable drift. Wife Jackie and I met Ken several miles above Belknap Springs. The river is faster up there, with more rocks, and harder to fish. This day was perfect! Jackie caught a 15-inch fish just minutes after we put in, and fishing improved from then on!

We could've caught a boatload of fish. I have fished that stretch almost every year with Ken, never again matching that first time. But our score there has been reasonable, thanks to remembering to REFLOAT!

Ever a beautiful river, the McKenzie no longer yields the bounty of yesteryear. Even so, the fishing remains fun and, equally enjoyable, the still-present wildness of the environs. Just remember, the key in hopes of catching McKenzie redsides, if that is your pleasure, is still that magic word—REFLOAT!

[1](For the uninitiated, refloating is use of a dropper fly, above the traditional terminal fly. By lifting the fly rod, the dropper refloats to the surface, normally with surprisingly good results. The technique is thought to have originated on the McKenzie.)

ON WADING DEEPER

Not surprisingly, the McKenzie River's role in popularizing fly-fishing amongst men, also helped introduce more women to the sport. While not the sole influence, there is clear evidence of how one singular "awakening" on that very river led to many, many others.

This story begins in the drift boat of Prince Helfrich during the military leave from WWII army duties of Walter Haas, Jr. His young wife, Evelyn, is content to accompany them with a book, rather than fly-rod, in her hands. Today, Mrs. Haas recalls:

"At some point ... on one of our early McKenzie trips ... I suddenly put down the book I was reading and announced:

'This is dumb! Starting NOW, I want to learn to fly-fish!'

"Well, everybody was so relieved at my decision, they all wanted to help. And that was the beginning of what took us to many places..."

And it was, also, the genesis of a little breakthrough book she co-authored in 1979 with a longtime fishing companion, Gwen Cooper. In being a guiding light for the project, Nick Lyons, wrote:

"I warmly hope that this book will herald a new era."

It did! "WADE A LITTLE DEEPER, DEAR" went through four printings and still is out of print. Until it appeared, virtually nothing on fly-fishing had been written by and for women.

Gwen Cooper waited until her family was raised before she started fly-fishing, but eventually found herself on the McKenzie and in a Helfrich drift boat. Still later, the book concept developed under interesting circumstances, as she explains:

"We had decided to try for an Atlantic Salmon and were in Labrador on the Eagle River. Our husbands were fishing and Evie and I were in the little tar paper shack overlooking the river when the idea came to us! Somehow on that trip, I ended up catching the largest salmon!"

She, like Mrs. Haas, however, is modest about her angling prowess. The latter explains her own metamorphosis and of women's' role in the sport, by observing:

"I think our patience is what brings us some success. The trout just finally get bored and strike! And if not, we have enjoyed being on the stream."

The "we" has sometimes included Justice Sandra Day O'Connor.

And the "stream" these days is at Beaver Meadows, out of Livingston, Montana, where she hopes her grandchildren will follow her lead.

Their husbands were college classmates and fly-fishermen while at Berkeley. The late Walter Haas went on to head up the family's Levi Strauss Co. empire. Joseph Cooper temporarily left the family's olive groves to develop an auto and equipment leasing business in San Francisco.

His fishing focus for the past two decades has been California's McCloud River and he has written a private edition of adventures there.

THE VALUE OF REVISITATION—Familiarity breeds success

Some folks constantly bound off to find new fishing, always assuming it will be better where they're going because it's not very good where they've been. This kind of thinking is excellent when fishing is truly bad. But it becomes a self-fulfilling prediction on water where the fishing could be excellent if only they'd stick around and fish the same place twice.

I thought about this when fishing Oregon's McKenzie River with Scott Richmond, author of the acclaimed Pocket Ghillie, ... just days after ... Scott had floated the river ... earlier with his publisher, Madelynne Sheehan, of Flying Pencil Publications.

(Dave Hughes was ready to end a no-fish day when Richmond remembered an unlikely stretch where Publisher Sheenhan earlier took three fish. He positioned Hughes into it, where a trout took—and kept—Dave's March Brown Comparadun and saved it from being a "skunk" day on the McKenzie.)

It's surprising how often fishing improves when you return to water that beat you up a little the first time you fished it. I'm not knocking the urge to gallop off elsewhere when fishing is not excellent where you're at. But try returning to a place where you've had just average fishing now and then, especially if it's beautiful.

Because of what you know the second time around, fishing will almost automatically be better. After that, you'll return again and again. And at each visitation, you'll learn a little more, and perhaps catch a few more or larger fish.

—Dave Hughes
ROD & REEL Magazine
January/February, 1996

RECOLLECTIONS OF A CHAT WITH CLARA DINKELSPIEL

May 2000

The first McKenzie River visit of John and Clara Dinkelspiel remains vivid in her mind because it was during a very hot spell in the summer of 1939.

They were there at the invitation of Cousins Jim and Elizabeth Gerstley, who in turn were staying in the guest cottage of an uncle, Harold Mack.

Mack had made a killing in the stock market and had "retired to fish" while still in his thirties. Mack's comfortable cottage was below Thomson's Lodge, also on the south side of the river. When it wasn't occupied by Mack or his guests, it sometimes was used as overflow lodging by Thomson guests.

As a result, Mack and the Thomsons, and especially Dayton, were on very good terms.

Milo Thomson was John and Clara's first guide. He placed them on a big rock, where they could fish a long run or riffle.

"I ... we ... didn't really know how to fish," Clara remembers. But they were with able mentors in Dayton and Milo Thomson.

They stayed a long week that first trip. They also fished with Dick and Cecil Byerly ... on the Santiam ... in the Detroit Reservoir area.

The following year, 1940, they also stayed at Mack's cottage. Their guide that year was Earl Jeans.

They also fished the Willamette twice that year.

From then on, they returned each summer, usually in mid-June, for two weeks, mostly to fish with Mac McMullin. Because John and his brother, were law partners, they never took fishing vacations at the same time.

The routine was to fish mornings until, say, 1 p.m.—take a midday break until 2:30 or 3 o'clock—and then fish until dark.

Favored wading places were at Finn Rock Flat ... near the Hawthorne/ Edgewood/Heaven's Gate area ... and on the South Fork, under the bridge. They were the Gerstley's favorites as well.

John and Clara were witnesses or near-witnesses to several tragic circumstances, including:

They were sitting on their porch when the search party for the bodies of Milo Thomson and his two clients drifted by ... three boats side by side across the river ... each with a searcher prone in the bow ... the oarsman ... and another searcher aft ...

There are two versions of the accident ... possibly a bit of each is true ... one is that Milo, a small oarsman, had two large dudes in his boat at Blue

River when one stood ... lurched forward and upset the boat - The other is that there had been alcohol involved during the float down river.

At end of one float with Mac McMullin, the boat was beached on the south riverbank while Mac crossed the bridge at Finn Rock Store where his truck was parked. Just minutes before, the shopkeeper of the store was murdered and, had Mac been a witness to the get-away, he might've been a victim as well.

There used to be a prominent fishing party headed by a Dan Stone and it was known as the "Stone Party." Stone was a friend of Uncle Mack. The Walter Haas family sometimes was a part of the Stone party.

Clara tells a story that personnel of a large WWII army camp in the Bend, OR, area come over and "cleaned out" a majority of the legal trout population in the McKenzie. Certainly, there was a dramatic drop in the quantity and quality of trout during that time.

(The explanation that I was given in my research was that during that period, the U.S. Forest Service did extensive DDT spraying in the upper McKenzie Valley watershed to curb a heavy spruce bud worm infestation. Fish biologists found many dead trout with stomachs filled with worms. That was when the push to protect the larger spawning trout began.

I do have written confirmation from the Forest Service of the DDT spraying. I very much doubt the U.S. Army is going to give me any confirmation that there was excessive overkill of McKenzie trout by greedy camp personnel.—Editor)

McKenzie River Days

By C. Dean Johnson

Mother and Dad were both excellent fly fishermen and they fished on the McKenzie. Their first trip was to Thomson's Lodge, just at the foot of Martin Rapids, on the south side of the river. The Thomsons had a river-powered ferry across the river, and that was the place to stay. From what I heard, their first trip was rather exciting.

The lodge fixed them up with a guide and they went up to McKenzie Bridge to put in the river. (That way they would get a good ride even if they didn't know how to fish.) Their boat was an ordinary rowboat which had a couple of boards mounted on the sides at the aft end to give a bit more freeboard. This was before the development of the McKenzie drift boats. Of course the McKenzie has an important tributary called Blue River, and is somewhat smaller above that point. McKenzie Bridge is several miles above Blue River and the river falls more rapidly, making the rapids shallower and faster. In addition to being exciting, at times it was also frightening and my parents never forgot it! It also came out later that it was the guide's first trip with paying dudes! His name was Prince Helfrich. He later became famous as one of the best, if not the very best, guides and organizers of great fishing trips. Many readers have ridden with him, his three sons, or his grandsons, all of whom have been premier guides and fishermen.

In the years that followed, the shape of the boats changed radically. First, they became flat bottomed with a lot of rake fore and aft. The stern was made much wider and the transom tipped so as to deflect the wave as they were let down through the fast water backward. This made them heavier but at least seaworthy in the fast water. These boats were often too heavy to manage safely with two passengers, especially when the passengers were big. Even then, many people walked around Martin Rapids and the boatman went through alone.

Since my Mother and Father liked to fish together, and they were both rather big, dad tried to design a boat suitable for the task. This was the time when U.S. Plywood had made the first marine plywood—plywood that would not delaminate in water. Super Hardboard, it was called. Dad built two boats out of the new plywood, each large enough for two good-sized men plus the oarsman. They were a great success. Though larger, they were lighter and handled quite well.

Dad also built a house trailer. It slept four, had electric lights, a stove, ice box, and water for a shower and toilet. During the fishing season, Mother had it loaded on Friday and after work Dad rushed home and we all jumped in the car and headed for the McKenzie.

We stayed at Dolly's Stockade at Clover Point. We rented and then bought a spot down near the river from Dolly. Dad rigged up a trailer hitch on the front of the car and we would drive in after dark, unhitch and turn the car around and push the trailer down into the black hole by the river. Dinner was a little late, but we were all ready for fishing the next morning.

At the same time, two great guides from the McKenzie were working as hand fallers in the woods out of Toledo. One was York Thomson (I think the oldest son of the Thomsons who owned the lodge), probably the best boatman on the McKenzie and a great fisherman. The other was John West, who also raised lilies on a place a few miles above the dam. They both took off from Toledo on Friday (or sooner) and were ready to row the next morning. York taught me how to handle the fast water and not a little about where the fish were hiding. John did the same and gave me hell when I missed a strike! I was twelve and "graduated" when I could get through Martin Rapids without shipping any water. Even had a few non-paying dudes after that!

JUDGE JIM CRAWFORD

BY DALE LAFOLLETTE
The Creel, Vol. 10, No. 1, June, 1973

We had spent the morning on Horse Creek. Fishing had been nil, but the judge had a thing about Horse Creek. He had fished there with his father; in fact, they had camped there when he was just a lad and he wanted to visit Horse Creek whenever we fished the McKenzie.

This day was dull and threatening and we started back to our cabin at McKenzie Bridge rather early. As we came to the Forest Service Building the judge asked me to stop there. We went in and found a large room half-filled with men in rough clothing, evidently waiting for something.

"I came in here," the judge said "to ask if any of you knew the origin of the name Horse Creek."

No one spoke up. So the judge went to the coke machine, got a couple of cokes, then asked, "Who was the McKenzie named for?"

No answer, but one fellow in uniform spoke up, "In case you wonder about all these men sitting idle, we anticipate an intense, dry electrical storm and have called them in as a precautionary measure in case we have a number of lightening strikes."

The judge passed a few pleasantries, we finished our cokes and left. That night sleeping on a cot in the living room I was awakened by a loud clap of thunder and the sound of pouring rain. Shortly, in the glow of the fireplace, appeared the judge, dressed in blue striped pajamas and waving one hand he said:

"We anticipate a dry electrical storm ..."

The judge usually spent two weeks on the McKenzie in August. The first few years we fished together there he would hang his mirror and toothbrush on a nail in a tree and drop his sleeping bag on the ground at a place on the bank about a mile west of McKenzie bridge. An excellent restaurant on the highway a short distance away took care of the food problem and the trees came out there above us, providing all the shelter we ever needed.

We would bring the newspaper back from breakfast and sit on the ground with our backs to a large tree and read it, once in awhile gazing out over the McKenzie, admiring the sun through the maple leaves. The judge, chewing on his pipe, would comment on the news or lack of it.

We would usually hike in the late morning and early afternoon, fish until an hour before dinnertime, then rendezvous with the Old Fitzgerald and cheese and crackers until the urge struck us to go to dinner.

On this occasion we had just returned to camp and washed up in the river and the judge was rummaging in the back of the station wagon for the Old Fitz, etc. He was on his knees in the front seat leaning over the back of it when he stopped and turned to me, his pipe in his mouth. Bending down so he could see me through the door he said, "Dale, things have come to a pretty pass when the cheese and crackers are in the same container as the dirty sox!"

We were camped at the base of the "after breakfast tree" that night in 1959 when the news came in over the radio that a landslide in Montana had buried so many people. We talked late that night.

The judge had trouble with his knees. Quite a few of his fishing trips were spoiled by knee trouble, and knees were about the only thing I ever heard him complain about.

I had lunch with him and Judge Martin Hawkins one time when the judge's knees were bothering him. He said to Hawkins, "Mart, you being an Olympic athlete and all, what do you suppose my knee trouble is?"

Hawkins frowned and thought awhile, then asked "You don't suppose walkin' on the damn things for 69 years has anything to do with it?"

The judge had been in a cabin at McKenzie Bridge for a week or two and I drove up to fish with him a few days and bring him home.

When I arrived he was limping, using a broken limb for a cane. He had fallen twice that morning, bruising a different knee each time. I cut him a cane and we took it easy. We drove rather than hiked, drifted the river rather than fish the bank as we usually did, and returned to Portland somewhat sooner than expected.

The following week the judge showed up for lunch with a stranger. He was an Eastern Oregon judge serving pro-tem in Multnomah County.

During lunch, Judge Crawford mentioned his crippled knees and the Eastern Oregonian asked what was wrong with them.

"A fish bit me," he said.

The Eastern Oregonian asked "What kind of fish was that?"

The answer was, "A damned mean fish!"

Recently I made a trip to the old campsite again and, in a manner of speaking, I took the judge. Mentally I talked to him all the way up the valley. I reviewed the many previous trips and smiled at his drolleries.

The river was unchanged. It plunged by the "after breakfast tree" with its usual urgency. The vista across the river was just as beautiful—just as restful—but it didn't satisfy.

I stayed quite awhile.

Then I left him there at the base of the "after breakfast tree."

Robert Pickering Arkley

Featured in The Creel of December 1964 was Robert Pickering Arkley's lifetime account of his saw milling and fly-fishing experiences from British Columbia to California. Here is his 1964 remembrance of days in McKenzie Country:

"I went to Oregon again in 1939 when my sawmill burned in South Bend, WA. I bought a sawmill in Eugene, and a home, and so forth. That's when I met Winkie Wentler, bless his heart. He's still up there. He was an enthusiastic fisherman and, oh, the damndest guy. We used to play golf together and we used to fish together and shoot together. He was a great joke to me, always. He would get excited and holler and yell. I would say, "You talk to me like that, Wink, and I'll throw you out of this damned boat!

"Wink had a McKenzie boat and trailer and we would go up the McKenzie and the Willamette. We encountered Mr. Hoover several times and spoke, nodded to him as we passed in the boat … but I never met him. He is a great McKenzie man. I never cared for the McKenzie, particularly. I like the Willamette very much better. We used to get some nice heavy fish up there, and there were easy to fish riffles. There was some fast water, but nothing terrible like Gate Creek Rapids and Martin Rapids. I wouldn't go through the Martin Rapids on a bet with any guide there is!

"Well, anyway, Wink and I used to fish all of that area – down on the Siuslaw, down on the Umpqua, up on the Willamette and the McKenzie, and the rest of the time, when I wasn't busy, we'd play golf out at the country club in Eugene. Yeh, he was a great guy … Winkie."

A Christmas tradition for generations in the Scottish Arkley clan was to get another fly rod. Greenhart was never Bob Arkley's favorite. Nor was an old dry fly Leonard given him by his Uncle John. He preferred wet fly action.

"One of my favorites, after graduating from Greenhart, was a Montague," he recalled. "Not a cheap Montague, but an expensive one I bought in Tacoma. It proved a marvelous rod when the only way you can learn to cast a fly is to cast a fly … lots of it … for a long time!"

Damsel Flies

During the Eighties, Bob Guard's late wife had organized and Dan Callaghan had incorporated the first women's FFF-affiliated club, called the Damsel Flies. After it became defunct, a new women's club—with the same name—was organized out of the Caddis Fly Shop.

The Damsel Flies include (from left) Karon Morgan, Joan McCreery, Lucille Jellison, Amy Fields and Dorothy Goode.

No one in present Damsel Flies' membership of forty-some was ever in the original club. And while there has never been a demonstrated strong entomological tie between natural caddis flies and natural damsel flies, one certainly exists between the fly shop and the women's club by those names! Damsel Flies get special attention and discounts there. They often are guided personally by Chris Daughters or someone else from his shop or by John Fabian, remembered nationally for his remarkable Scientific Angler video tapes. And when a float tube outing is planned by Damsel Flies, those who don't have that equipment get loaners from the shop.

Of many outings with Daughters, one described in detail by Dorothy Goode, an articulate spokesperson for her Damsel Fly sisters, is memorable for having involved Jessica Maxwell, who wrote I Don't Know Why I Swallowed The Fly. Says Goode:

"Jessica, as a member, invited us to utilize her parent's place on the McKenzie, a property to die for! Chris furnished guides with boats for eight of us for what we called our "Trout & Tea" trip in the summer of '98. Jessica had arranged we fish down to her parent's place, take out there and each read a favorite fly fishing passage while having tea and goodies, and then fish a little while longer.

"We all caught fish, I think. I know I caught a 24-inch rainbow, but who's measuring!"

Most Damsel Flies concentrate on the McKenzie and the Willamette, but some more venturesome fly—and fish—far afield. They range in age from early twenties to Lucille Jellison, who broke down her rod the last time upon reaching ninety. But, not before a weeklong trip to the Bighorn River in Montana in 1995, and a weekend trip to Oregon's Crooked River out of Prineville that same concluding season.

Damsel Flies' adventures and resulting anecdotes have been manyfold. So far, their 15 minutes of fame have been ephemeral. Two local TV station cameramen followed eight of them streamside for two hours of taping—which ended up as a 90-second spot on the evening news.

Damsel Flies wade more than fish from drift boats. And when they choose boating, Guide Fabian most often is their choice. Fabian does not consider himself a McKenzie pioneer though he has fished it for almost fifty years. When he started in 1955, his mentors were George and Charlie Logan and longtime fly tier and guide, Bill Hunt.

Interested women can find out more from the e-mail address: oregondamselflies@hotmail.com

Jackie Coveny

How Jacque "Jackie" Coveny came to be a "hostess with the mostest" among upper river residents and visitors near and far becomes evident as she enthuses in wonderment and thankfulness of how it used to be-- and still is, thanks to her positive personality.

A fourth generation Californian (her great grandmother was born coming to California in a covered wagon), Jackie grew up in small town circumstances she says make her "... fit right in" during her annual six months at her waterside retreat. That extensive time frame allows for much socializing as well as fishing and golfing. Often, however, fishermen are absent from frequent cocktail parties-- they're still fishing!

Her breathtaking vista at waterside summer home, Rillerah, most often is alive with the sound of voices of angling and other friends. (Older readers will recall the WWII era tune, "... hut sut on the Rillerah." It was popular when Jackie acquired her McKenzie place 32 years ago. Jackie:

"I think I'm one of the few ladies you'll meet on the upper river who did not learn to flyfish through her father or husband. A kind of 'adopted uncle,' Frank Bennett, exposed me to the sport on Montana's Madison and Gallatin rivers after my husband, Carleton, died in 1973." In her charming open manner, Jackie volunteers that she wasn't very good to start and evolved slowly with the help of many mentors.

Jackie:

"I spent a great deal of time trying to stop my rod at ten o'clock and avoid a low backcast. More recently I learned that I was losing the big ones by not letting them take me to the reel. So, to this day, when setting out in a drift boat, I always ask my guide to tell me what I'm doing wrong!"

The late Frank Brown, her first licensed guide and former wholesale foods dealer, was a good teacher. So was Ennis Nestle, who figured in one of her highlight days astream. Jackie: "It was a real thrill to catch a steelhead on a dry yellow caddis pattern with my little (8-foot, 2 1/4 oz) Orvis graphite rod! Then, to catch yet another steelhead on a wet fly that same trip!"

She credits still other "gentlemen/flyfishermen" ... and ladies ... with her metomorphisis into a journeyman angler. They included the late Alan Chickering, an early member of our Oregon flyclub; John Hooker, Ben Charles and Pauline Fischer Chickering. Of those experiences Jackie comments:

"Everyone became so excited and helpful when I was taking up the sport. To this day I find it my pleasure to see younger people advancing as I did. They must feel as I did when, after catch-and-release of a big fish, I'd call friends between here and London!"

Now and then some of Jackie's earlier trips were with Wayne Price who roomed with Frank Brown. Today, she fishes mostly with Price's grandson, Greg White, and with Wade Thomas, more recently an active guide. Jackie:

"Greg and I kind of grew up together as far as fishing goes. He's one of those wonderful people I revere who live here and who taught me to have respect for the beauty and the bounty of this place. And, of course, the right way to fish!"

After her husband's death and she was alone at Rillerah, she promised everyone she wouldn't wade McKenzie waters unassisted. She points out that those who do, no matter how sure-footed, have a healthy respect for the river and use wading staffs without apology. Jackie:

"A friend who died in 1998 often ventured into a wonderful wading place just upstream from here ... right out in the middle! Good strong waders also find fish right out in front of Rillerah!"

Her husband's priorities were golf and his own business, including a career as a music lyrics writer, an ASCAP composer. Small wonder that Jackie knew music and musicians. When Harry Owens, composer of "Sweet Lalani" and other Hawaiian standards died, she started his widow, Helene Owens Jones of Eugene toward drift boat fishing. Jackie:

"So now, for my October birthday, Helene every year gives me a present of an extra fishing trip up the river, quite as much as I did for her when she was widowed!"

Jackie makes her positions on issues of the river quite clear. In spite of strong feelings of San Francisco friends, she doesn't think the upper McKenzie should be " ... a totally fly-only river." Jackie:

"Think about it. I know people up here who need to eat some of the fish they catch. Y'know, not everyone is in a position to hire a guide with a driftboat at the present (1999) rate of $235 per day!"

And barbless flyhooks? Jackie again:

"Well, it if was my decision, I'd be using barbless! But then the guides I know are so careful with hooked fish that I don't worry when I fish with them. That included the late Merl McMullin, a great guide and a fine man. And, a rule unto himself !"

Jackie's position on barbless likely was reinforced afloat when:

"I cast too fast into a wind and hooked my chin! Ted Bryant wrapped a piece of leader around the shank and pressed down and popped that flyhook out ever so easily. All I had was a tiny pin prick! I think that guides know how to take a hook out better than most doctors.

Originally, golf at Tokatee brought the Covenys from Palm Springs to the upper McKenzie. They had planned a vacation home in Provence, France, but the deal fell through and Ben Charles suggested they rent a little log cabin on the back of one of his extensive properties in order to look around. Jackie:

"It was just a one-room affair, so small that a notch had been cut into the 'John's' seat so the bathroom door could open and close! Even so, we enjoyed six weeks of golf and the beauty of the river and decided to buy here."

In Palm Springs, where Jackie was a party-giving consultant, friends learned of their new summer home on the McKenzie, and there was a considerable increase in golfers and anglers from California. And from Pacific Northwest friends as well -- the late Meg and Anson Brooks of Seattle; the late Ted Lilley and his wife, Joanne, of Portland; Bob Noyes and Spencer Ehrman as well. Brooks, Lilley and Ehrman all longtime Oregon flyclub members. Jackie:

"One of my younger friends who has taken up flyfishing on this river is Mrs. Dodel (Nancy) Fischer whose husband is the son of the late Dale Fischer of Far West Steel, Eugene. They now have a place, as well, at Camp Sherman on the Metolious.

Prominent Oregon lumbermen Wil Gonyea of Roseburg and Nat Giustina of Eugene figured in McKenzie affairs. Giustina was a major force in starting and developing Tokatee golf course."

Jackie recalls a bygone era when the late Edna (Mrs. Blair) Rukker fished the McKenzie. As a child in San Francisco, she would come north by train to Eugene then take stagecoach over McKenzie Pass to Black Butte Ranch, owned by her parents, to spend summers. Jackie:

"Later, Edna and her husband used to come to the McKenzie and stay at Loloma Lodge. They acquired a little house there. Some folks have referred to that part of our neighborhood as the 'Gold Coast'."

While Jackie's Rillerah has two bedrooms for guests, she is adding yet another. Jackie:

"My house guests always hope to receive an honorary membership certificate in the McKenzie River Guides Association.

"My kitchen walls and cabinets are plastered with certificates and photos of happy fishing guests. They consider it an honor to be here. And I consider it an honor to have them!"

Dr. Dick's Magical McKenzie Remedy

By Lenox Dick, M.D.

In 1962 when I took over as the Benson Hotel's house doctor, it included the care of a Mr. Goldberg. He was well over 80 and had suffered a stroke, rendering his left side so weak he could not walk unassisted. When I visited Mr. Goldberg in his dark and dreary suite, his live-in nurse told me, "Mr. Goldberg is very depressed and cried all night. It doesn't help that the hotel management wants him to move elsewhere. He keeps saying, 'I want to die, I want to die'. Dr. Dick, he is definitely suicidal!"

I assured Mr. Goldberg that my treatment of his bladder infection would make him feel better. And I said I would talk to the manager about staying in the hotel. (He had been a permanent resident since the 30s, when many grand hotels needed to fill rooms.) He seemed to perk up some at that. Then I noticed a beautiful mount of a large, bright rainbow trout.

"Wow," I exclaimed, "Mr. Goldberg, did you catch that magnificent trout?"

He perked up a bit more and responded: "Yes, Doctor, on the McKenzie River many years ago, and on a McKenzie Special fly, too."

The memory of the moment improved his attitude further as he continued:

"There was a big hatch of McKenzie caddis that day. When I saw that very trout rise, I cast to him. He took my McKenzie and I had to play him almost twenty minutes before Milo landed him. Yes, Milo Thomson, the guide. He told me it was the biggest rainbow anyone had caught that year."

He had stayed at the old Thomson's Lodge and recalled the tragedy of Milo drowning with two California clients in his boat in the Blue River rapids. So I told him how in 1947 my father in law, Spencer Biddle, had introduced me to Milo as our guide for a day on the McKenzie. I remembered him as a small, wizened old man in his late sixties or seventies. His skin was as yellow as a pumpkin, causing me, with my new-found medical knowledge, to whisper to Mr. B:

"That man has advanced cirrhosis of the liver. He can't possibly row us all day!"

But to my surprise he not only rowed us all day, he rowed very well. His skills enabled us to catch many trout. After Milo drowned, his family put his ashes in a silver urn and sank it in the Finn Rock pool. It is said that if you go through that pool and pour a bit of Scotch into the water, Milo's silver urn will bob to the surface. Like Mr. Goldberg, I too missed Milo.

Mr. Goldberg had brightened considerably during discussion of his big fish, but at mention of Milo he started to sob despondently on his bed. I quickly changed the subject, announcing that I would go immediately to talk with the hotel manager. Neither Mr. Goldberg nor the manager knew I had an ace to play.

Mr. Goldberg's favorite nephew, Morrie, was an up-and-coming, no-nonsense trial lawyer and a fishing friend of mine. He was very fond of the old man, in part because he had financed his Willamette Law School studies. I advised the hotel manager that if there was a move to evict his uncle, Morrie would secure a restraining order, sending the issue to court. There, I said, I would testify that making him move would kill him.

While the manager digested that news, I raised another issue. Part of Mr. Goldberg's depression probably stemmed from the gloomy, dingy appearance of his suite, which had not been redecorated since his arrival there in the thirties. The manager countered that during the Depression such an expenditure was impossible, and now the hotel needed the space to produce more income. But he said he would do nothing until he had consulted the hotel's owners.

When I returned to Mr. Goldberg with that news, he was sitting in his wheelchair, despondently eating breakfast. I prescribed some of the mood elevating drugs that had just come on the market.

Mr. Goldberg's mood did perk up, to the point that he would occasionally allow his nurse to hire a limousine for drives in the country. I then suggested those drives be to small rivers close to Portland where roads paralleled the streams. The nurse reported later that he began to have the driver stop opposite a pool or riffle and exclaim:

"See that rock. I bet there's a steelhead or a big trout behind it." Or "Look, there are mayflies hatching. This time of year they should be March Browns."

Steadily the drugs and his trips afield helped his progression out of his depression. And the eviction problem was resolved. The Benson did not want to tangle with nephew Goldberg.

Lunching one day with Morrie I suggested we send his uncle, nurse and limousine further afield, down to the McKenzie for a few days. Morrie agreed immediately. He had been negotiating to have his uncle's quarters redecorated in brighter colors, at his expense. He then went to see see his uncle and said:

"Uncle, you are going back to the McKenzie, this time at Riverview Lodge, where the porch extends over the river and you can dap a fly for trout. While you are away, your rooms will be redecorated."

The next morning, with the help of the driver and nurse, the trip south began. After a few days I called the lodge to ask the nurse how things were going.

"Well, he cried most of the way down," she reported, "but perked up and started to point out various landmarks along the river, remembering Finn Rock, Silver Creek, Rennie's Rapid, and so on. And when I wheeled him out on the lodge porch, he really perked up."

She explained how the cook had set up the rod and reel I'd sent along. Mr. Goldberg had chosen a McKenzie Special, of course, which the cook (a fly fisher herself) had tied to his leader. He let line out, dapping his fly onto the waters below until hooking a trout. As it flopped onto the porch, the cook took it off the hook, and Mr. Goldberg's silent smile turned into outright laughter.

"I have never seen such a change in a patient in my life," the nurse exclaimed. "He hooked two more smaller trout that got away, but the cook fried the first one for his breakfast."

That report pleased me and encouraged the next step in Mr. Goldberg's therapy afield. Knowing Merl McMullin from earlier trips, I phoned him and asked if he could take Mr. Goldberg down the river. He agreed and explained the he had taken wheelchair anglers fishing in the past by bolting onto his boat two armchairs with the legs cut off. And so a float trip was arranged for two mornings later. The following evening I just had to find out how it went. Mac reported:

"Pretty tough at first. He thought you were crazy to have arranged it, and just might consider firing you as his doctor. I didn't argue, just continued telling some of my best river stories, which got him laughing. Finally he gave in and the limo driver helped get him and the nurse into those armchairs."

McMullin was pleased to learn that Mr. Goldberg knew all about the float/refloat method of fishing a fly on the McKenzie. He had not forgotten the lessons Milo Thomson had taught him years earlier. McMullin continued:

"Doc, it was one of those days when the McKenzie Specials were all over the water. When Mr. Goldberg wondered if he still could reach the hot spots because of his arthritis, I told him to just let out line, holding the rod tip high enough for dapping. I held and maneuvered the boat back and forth. We did this on every riffle we came to and released about twenty fish.

"What a change came over that man! He laughed and cheered. At lunchtime I managed to carry him to a log, where he watched while I fried up a mess of keeper fish. Boy, how he and that nurse worked those fish over."

McMullin reported they'd be on the water again for the next three days.

When Mr. Goldberg returned to his redecorated suite, he was a new man. He frequently went out in the limo to movies, plays and other public places. He visited his few surviving old friends. He traveled to Palm Springs for the worst of his remaining winters.

Mr. Goldberg enjoyed those new patterns in his life until he died in his sleep, three fishing seasons later. I have written lots of prescriptions, but that was one of my very best.

McKenzie Gifts

By Steve Arndt

It was the coldest, clearest water I had ever almost drowned in, as I recall my introduction to the McKenzie River in September of 1967. It was an innertube trip with the University of Oregon freshman swim team. The hole in Martin's Rapids had relieved me of my craft, and three separate efforts up for air had failed. Eventually, a helpful surge of water, heading in one direction instead of recycling, picked me up and shot me out of that hydraulic. Looking like a half-drowned blue rat I made it to safety and was grateful. Lesson? Just because the water gets through does not insure safe passage for humans or their craft.

I explored the McKenzie and some of its tributaries and reservoirs for the balance of what proved to be colorful Eugene years. I did find a run, marked by the confluence of a tributary, where even I, a rat-whiskered hippie dog, could catch a fish.

Colors change in the river with the slant of the sun. From steel gray to turquoise. It runs swiftly over bright gravel bars, sweeps over round boulders, swirls around lava outcroppings, and occasionally slows enough to mirror the blue sky and sunlit mountains of forest and cliff. Then, often following a quiet moment, the river as seen from the pool above, disappears and all that can be seen is vapor and spray. All that can be heard is thunder.

Each rapid has its own way of being defiant. The entrance, usually a slick green tongue that rolls and spills at its tip, is the last organized moment the water has. The wet chaos can now manifest itself in a number of varying hydraulic pronouncements as the riverbed attempts to manage the unmanageable. They are beautiful creations of a mystifying Mother Earth and we are compelled to be in awe of them.

I guided for seven years for Dave Helfrich. Before my first trip on the Middle Fork he called me and suggested I come down and float the Upper McKenzie with his son Ken. The upper river flows almost non-stop like the Middle Fork and provides similar challenges. So the following weekend we made my training trip into a cookout outing.

I met Ken along with the others at Ollalie Campground, our put-in. They had already spotted cars downriver at McKenzie Bridge. I had no passengers, just food, firebox and libations. No rods either, since up this high the waters are restricted for spawning. The stream here is only about a third the size down near Vida Bridge. The current never slows into pools. As on the Middle Fork, a boatman is constantly busy positioning.

The rapid of note on this stretch is known as the Fishladder. We scouted this one from a high bank. There were varying opinions on which approach to take and what cuts needed to be made. Fishladder is a boulder patch in an elongated "S" shape. It drops quickly, it's fast with rocks to dodge and eddies to catch to help slow the boat, and a serious cut to the right at the bottom end. One of those necessary cuts to keep from high-centering on rocks (One the size of a Volksvagen) which can top and fill a boat in a cold second. Ken and I watched two boats make it through successfully. Despite a couple of loud, vibrating bangs which aluminum boats are famous for, Ken was confident we had picked the right channel. I joined Ken in his boat for this effort, which went flawlessly, without noise except for the growl and snarl of the water, punctuated by oarlocks and oars.

Here was that feeling, that time out before you go out on the floor to attempt the game-winning free throw. Walking back to your boat, alone in your thoughts after scouting rapids never seen before. Knowing that downriver the proven ones, your peers, are waiting for the nose of your boat to appear around the bend, and begin your initial approach. I'm life-jacketed and just ready to shove off when I hear a voice and spot Ken coming my way, saying he is riding with me. The thought of an extra 170 pounds doesn't even reach the conscious. I am more confident now with Ken aboard, and we make it through nice and neat, with only a slightly detectable metallic moment that only we hear. We join the others at the bottom, receiving their hoots of approval. I do my best to almost yawn and a hummmm, "What's next" look.

I will never forget the miles of river that passed under my boat, nor the stories that unfolded in the years I shared with Dave Helfrich and his gifted crew. I am proud to have been a small part of a legacy that began with a few men on the McKenzie, early in the century. It was handed down with each generation as they continue to enrich the tradition.

My last intimacy with the McKenzie was several years ago when I hired Ken to take son Steve (8) and daughter Jenny (14) and me on a trout fishing excursion from Helfrich Landing down to Leaburg Lake. Somehow, I got "Helfriched" into doing a good part of the rowing. In truth, it was good to feel the oars against the water. It was hot that day but the fish were biting fast enough to keep the attention of my kids. Ken found some shade and cooked our trout McKenzie style over the fire, and told us about his rattlesnake bite on last year's Middle Fork season. Then back to the fishing. Me at the oars, Ken up front keeping Steve and Jenny busy with fish, and fielding non-stop questions about rattlesnakes.

C H A P T E R 5

SPECIAL PLACES

Photo by Dan Callaghan

"At least once, every Western angler should float-fish the upper McKenzie River in a McKenzie River drift boat and fish for McKenzie River rainbow trout. This would be a classic trip in a classic boat for classic fish."

ED PARK

OREGON EDITOR, OUTDOOR LIFE, MAY 1992

INMAN'S HOLIDAY FARM

Holiday Farm remains a historic must-see place for anglers, golfers and nature lovers despite the myriad physical changes and ownerships since stagecoach days. Other early landmarks have gone by the wayside due to fire, flood, etc. And though periodic major floods have rearranged the present McKenzie River Drive area, there remains a strong sense of permanence at Holiday's main lodge and satellite outbuildings.

Lane County historian Leroy B. Inman provides an early and interesting look at the lay of the land around Holiday Farm in his "Beautiful McKenzie," (South Fork Press, Roseburg, OR, 1996.)

Vivian Wright, recent owner of Holiday Farm.

Once James Belknap, first upper river settler, chose a future homestead site near a meandering channel in 1869. Mother Nature had the upper hand. Floods cut through the westerly part of Belknap Ranch, overflowing low places. More recent major floods have been changing the river back toward present-day flows. Inman sums it up:

"The land lying immediately north across the McKenzie River from James and Ella Belknap's original homestead at what today is known as Rainbow or Holiday Farm has an interesting history."

Interesting indeed! Names of physical places in the area changed as often as the settlers involved. Carey W. Thomson in 1878 built John Craig's bridge, which became McKenzie Bridge. He also built a bridge with his name, replacing James Belknap's ferry. That bridge later was known as Campbell's Bridge, then Belknap's Bridge.

But, what of those more directly responsible for Holiday Farm? And, was it, indeed, an early stagecoach stop? Historian Inman doesn't think so, even though certain Forest Service records show it built in 1876 as a stagecoach stop. Subsequent newspaper accounts echo that claim. Inman has good reason to believe that Thomas Trotter of Maple Valley, WA, and his family built the original structure about 1909 or 1910. Walden and Elva (Belknap) Trotter had filed homestead rights on the present site about 1908. Two years later, the Trotters built and occupied the house, which also served as a stage stop for several years. In 1922, following a divorce, Trotter sold the property to Lewis Quimby of Portland. Quimby sold to a man named Barrows, but by the early Forties the property belonged to a foursome of Forbes. Inman:

"The Forbes had operated the original Holiday Farm a mile east of Blue River on the McKenzie River Highway. When the building on that property was destroyed by fire, the Forbes acquired the Quimby property and moved their Holiday Farm business there."

Inman's family played major roles in the development of the area, and he

Paul Bourgault Watercolor

retains vivid memories of his boyhood roles. Inman:

"Quimby specialized in trout dinners in his restaurant. He put in pools by damming Mill Creek, which ran through the back of the farm, and stocked them with eastern brook ... customers would catch the fish in the ponds themselves, or could be supplied from a large freshwater tank on the front porch of his store/restaurant. Quimby would net fish from the ponds and put them in the tank. A fish dinner cost one dollar, no matter how taken.

"As a teenager, at Quimby's permission and request, I used to fish the ponds to supply the fish tank. Some of the trout had grown to a length of twenty inches or more and were a menace to the smaller fish.

"These larger fish were my objective!"

TOKATEE GOLF COURSE

"And on the eighth day, God hit a three-iron stiff to the pin on the 11th hole at Tokatee. And even if he three-putted, God couldn't get angry because even He had to be overwhelmed by what he had created."—Blaine Newnham, *Register-Guard Sports Editor, Summer 1971*

Actually, Tokatee had two epochal beginnings—the first in glacial times and the next in a more contemporary era. Today, the breathtaking mountain panorama continues to attract appreciative golfers as much as the nearby McKenzie River brings flyfisherfolk of the world to its banks.

No one is better backgrounded on Tokatee than Nat Giustina, prominent Eugene lumberman, who developed and named what has been called one of the fifty best public courses in America. There are only several glacial boulders now hardly noticeable on the fairways to remind of the beginnings. They were not disturbed during course development, and today still remind discerning players of an era which marked the end of a glacier's advance in the McKenzie Valley. A timbered morain ridge borders the course's right side.

Dan Callaghan photo

The few changes today are not glacial in nature. They do, however, present ongoing maintenance challenges. Fast-growing Douglas Fir, once they're obstructing the magnificent view of the Three Sisters mountain peaks to the east, are trimmed or taken down completely. The panoramic view of the lovely Sisters is, after all, Tokatee's crown jewel!

The Giustina family used to horseback into the Three Sisters Wilderness area for camping and fishing the high lakes. Tokatee Lake became a favorite. Giustina:

"The story is that Tokatee, in Cherokee, is 'pretty' or 'beautiful'. No visitor questions the meaning, nor likely even the stated origin."

Giustina's focus on his hobbies of the moment eventually led to the development of Tokatee. Earlier, he was deeply involved in hothouse agronomy. Golf hooked him during winter visits south to Thunderbird in the desert. Today, tethered by emphysema apparatus, genealogy by computer is his passion. His memories of Tokatee's beginnings are mint-bright. Giustina:

"When we became interested in the property for a golf course, cattle still were pastured in a large open space. Evidently the clearing had been used as a stopover place by the Indians traveling between eastern Oregon and the valley. We found arrowheads there and, at a windy point nearby, were piles of obsidian chips. Steady strong breezes at the point apparently kept pesky mosquitoes off the busy arrowhead makers."

After the Indian era, Boston Timber Company owned the land, then local Belknap Lumber Company logged the area. That further opened up country and provided pasturage for a Sims family's dairy farm. At one time, a fox farm operated there, and some still refer to that locality by that name.

By degrees, the Giustinas were moving upriver from their Eugene base to ultimate ownership of Tokatee property. Giustina:

"In '54 we bought the upriver place of W.E. 'Buck' Travis, founder of the Greyhound bus company. There were several cabins involved, including the 'Hoover Cabin' where the president once stayed. A loquacious lawyer once wrote Hoover a two-page letter asking if he remembered the writer's grandfather and if Hoover actually had stayed in the cabin named for him. From his suite in the Waldorf Towers, Hoover's response was a two-liner: 'Yes, I remember your grandfather. Yes, I stayed in that cabin.'"

Tokatee was on the drawing board after the minimum 160 acres were acquired and the acreage grew to 380 for possible residential development, which never came to pass. Construction began in 1964 and the front nine opened in '66. The second nine opened in 1970. A trailer and several small outbuildings still serve as a rustic complex.

Even so, the first longtime pro, Mickey Sullivan, once kept track of out-of-state golfers attracted to Tokatee. They represent 37 states! Oregon provides the greatest play, of course, followed by nearby California. Of all of yesterday's—and today's—visitors, Dixie Monkhouse, whose fly-fishing endurance also is legendary and chronicled elsewhere, has seen it all. Dixie:

"About 1965 we were taking our then current poodle on our favorite pasture walk when we saw some backhoe activity in the distance. We bustled over to see who was doing what to our special place! There we met Nat who told us of his Tokatee dream. Through the years, we watched his dream come true–one of the most beautifully maintained courses you'll ever see!"

Dixie speaks with gratitude of the ongoing friendship with the Giustina family and the courtesies extended by Tokatee staff over all those years, including always allowing the current poodle to make the rounds with the Monkhouse players. Dixie:

"In 1999 when sixteen of my family came up to celebrate my 90th, we had a Family Scramble – all of us! Even those who had never held a club before! On the first tee, I had to be the first off. As I addressed my ball, over the clubhouse loudspeaker blasted 'Happy Birthday, dear Dixie!'"

McKENZIE LANDMARKS

Many visitors to the McKenzie have remembered specific places and people along its banks more vividly than the river itself. Often their memories were of interesting places in which they had eaten or slept or both. And they included fly-fisher folk as much as the general public. Here, from "memory lane," are some notable examples not expressly cited elsewhere in this journal:

Paul Bourgault Watercolor

Sparks Ranch, probably the oldest structure still standing in Blue River, was home to a hotel, icecream parlor, and general store. Later became Blue River Inn, in early 60s remodeled as an apartment house.

Foley Hot Springs—Once Dr. Abram Foley acquired an interest in the mineral waters in 1870, he began development which extended through several ownerships until destroyed by fire in 1981. The emphasis was on fishing prospects as much therapeutic values. The McKenzie tributary, Horse Creek, was openly touted as " ... one of the most famous trouting streams in Oregon."

Foley's between years are most remembered for the iron rule of Ella Haflinger (1860-1950) whose strong will created a "Mrs. Hell-flinger" myth. Especially among young unmarried couples seeking overnight accommodations. Yet today a softer side of the indomitable matriarch is remembered as well. Mrs. Betty Alder, Hood Canal, WA, recalls how Mrs. Haflinger provided employment for a great uncle and a brother during lean years. And she, a wee girl, was befriended by the matriarch who gave her a rare bone china plate from her extensive collection and signed her "My Schoolday Autobiography" album " ... with love, to Betty Ann ..."

Paul Bourgault Watercolor

At turn of century, trout limit was 75 per day per person! Springfield museum photograph was used as artist's reference.

Betty Alder:

"I can still see my Dad setting out for Horse Creek, or the nearby McKenzie. His fly-bedecked felt hat was pulled low, his hip boots were folded down, his wicker creel and his jacket were stuffed with sandwiches, and a coffee thermos. Dad was a morning 'til dark fisherman."

As a North Carolinian from eastern hill country, Ross V. Moffitt depended upon fish and game to supplement the family larder. Betty:

"Our little rental cabin was apart from the main lodge, and in our independence there a wood fire stove would heat a heavy cast iron skillet and fry fresh trout, rolled in cornmeal and flour and seasoned only with salt and pepper."

Thomson's Sportsman Lodge—A teenager when his parents settled on the river's south side, across from Vida in 1870, Carey Thomson's pioneering energies eventually had locals calling him the "McKenzie River Iron Man." From market hunting for Eugene and Springfield outlets, among other outdoor income activities, he in 1900 built and operated the lodge which became famous in far-off fishing and hunting circles.

"He was the first man to take fishermen down the river in a boat for a fee," according to McKenzie historian, Leroy B. Inman. "They built an addition so the lodge could hold fourteen overnight guests."

The busy family staff included four sons, who operated the lodge after 1923. Milo, said to be the first guide to run Martin Rapids and, after a half-century

Paul Bourgault Watercolor

Seymor's Chateau was built in 1930 next to old fish hatchery on Leaburg Pond. Popular for meals, boating, fishing; burned in 1961.

of McKenzie boating, drowned in that very water with two fishing clients. Carey, Jr. (1909-1974) died of a heart attack while visiting Yellowstone Park. Dayton (1897-1974) was longtime manager of Thomson's. York (1902-1979) by 1940 had given up river guiding.

Thomson's hosted many Oregon flyclub members during its existence including the late C. Edwin Francis who once recalled fishing memories with his dad, Clarence E. Francis:

"I was just a kid when Dad decided I should run Martin Rapids. He went ashore at the rapids' head, and let me go through with our guide. I remember those waves looked BIG over our drift boat's gunwhales! Dad apparently had wanted it to make an impression on me. Which it did! I was grateful when we swung under the old swinging bridge and into Thomson's Landing."

The Thomson guiding dynasty sold the enterprise in 1948. It burned in 1954 and was never replaced.

The Wayfarer Resort—Once Thomson's and other early inns had disappeared, many McKenzie regulars shifted to more modern facilities, including Wayfarer, reached by crossing Goodpasture Bridge to the south side.

Among them was the traditional father-son opening day group of Len/Hugh Dick, Ed/Win Francis, Spencer/Spencer, Jr. Ehrman, and

Paul Bourgault Watercolor

If headed upriver, Davis & Korfs, one of the first gas stations on McKenzie, was a necessary stop.

Charlie/Eddie Miller. While Wayfarer offers spacious common facilities, this group gravitated to several of 13 private, fully applianced cabins for their opening day ceremonies and celebrations. Ehrman:

"We do our own cooking, which is surprisingly excellent. Len's wife, Helene, always sends a rhubarb pie which is wonderful."

Win Francis remembers that they called the season's opener "OD Day" for more than just one reason:

"In the hours of horseplay and pranks, away from focus on fishing, regulars were accorded new names. Among them, Doctor Dick became 'Doctor Gloom' and Marty Rathje became 'Basil Rathbone'."

Nothing personal, of course!

Phil's Phine Phoods—a popular eatery from 1944 until 1959 when success necessitated cutting back and operating only the growing grocery/hardware/lumber/gift shop complex, until it burned of incendiary origin in mid-1993. Clara Phillips, one of the owners, as quoted in the EUGENE REGISTER-GUARD:

"Business drew a lot of highfalutin' people, including stripper Gypsy Rose Lee and Clark Gable. Herbert Hoover used to get his fishing licenses from us."

Rustic Skillet—Also became popular with visitors and locals of the community of Rainbow for home cooking specialties served family style.

Cascade Resort—A recreation vehicle park now occupies the site of one of the most ambitious private resort projects ever attempted on the upper McKenzie in the mid-Twenties.

1918 photo of Clarence Francis and A. B. Smith, both Portland auto dealers, at Cook's McKenzie Inn.

Owners built a store, several cabins, a swimming pool, baseball diamond and other recreational facilities. During the Fifties, new owners built the Patio Cafe and installed a trailer court. The Patio burned in the early Sixties.

Wycoff Ranch—an early horse-changing station for eastbound stages, became Cook's Ranch when purchased by the Al Cook family. Between those times, it had been known to visiting angler and local alike as Sheppard's Ranch and still later as Heaven's Gate.

During the Cook's ranch era, Clarence E. Francis, with companions, was a regular there.

Belknap Springs—the Belknap family's almost feudalistic control of early access to the South Fork was relatively short-lived when in mid-1875 the property sold. A succession of owner-developers followed until a Michigan timber baron acquired the property and operated the resort for more than half a century.

The original developer, Roland Simeon Belknap, first had simple cabins, used as steam baths, for hunting parties he guided. Records indicate he built a hotel on the McKenzie's south side, "... on a beautiful level, tree-shaded bench. A daughter, Dora, augmented the arboreal splendor by planting maple trees when she was just twelve.

Nimrod (or Anglers) Inn—Longtime river boatman John West once described the establishment as the " ... high spot in the country ... and the place to go for Sunday dinners."

Originated by Alfred L. Parkhurst and taken over by William (Billy) Riley Price, the inn was pictured in a 1928 pamphlet as:

" ... a rustic building with a massive cobblestone fireplace in the lounge, a rustic dining hall, hot and cold running water, baths, and other modern plumbing and electric lights ... also boats available for anglers."

The Giddings—A 20-year dream came true for Charles and Lillian Mae Giddings and children in 1936 when they moved from Los Angeles to the McKenzie they had discovered on a vacation trip. Initially based in a marginal, deserted shack at Belknap Bridge, the Giddings, with local carpentry, built a home and a store and, eventually, four cabins. Historian Leroy Inman reports:

"They operated the store during the summer months., but there was little activity during the winter. They added a lunch counter, sold sandwiches, hamburgers, homemade pies and sometimes served meals to hungry, cold fishermen."

About Paul Bourgault: *One of the bonuses of on-site research is sometimes finding more than you had bargained for. Such was the case at the McKenzie River home of Marjorie Goodpasture who, when taking a breather from providing anecdotes of guiding experiences of husband and son, pointed out family photos around the room. Amongst them, an attractive watercolor card of an early-day scene along the McKenzie caught our eye. Sufficiently so that we tracked down the artist, Paul Bourgault, then living in Springfield with his wife Marguerite. One thing led to another and he graciously gave permission for us to reprint some of his works in our McKenzie journal.*

Paul Bourgault, was born and raised in New Hampshire and studied art and graphics in the East and Midwest until service in the U.S. Army Corps of Engineers brought westward to Hawaii. In Southern California he established and operated his own design and advertising agency until he and Marguerite sought a better quality of life in Oregon's Lane County and he seriously took up watercolor painting.

They now live in Elmira at 89476 Territorial Road and can be reached either by phone at (541) 935-2115 or E-mail Bourgy@mindspring.com.

DOWN BY THE RIVERSIDE

Many the McKenzie hostelry has been utilized for customer relations, but few other than the Wayfarer first, then later Riverside Lodge had been employed specifically for those purposes by a business. Not, that is, until a stevedoring partnership begun in San Francisco Bay shifted to Portland in 1951. To this day, although business use no longer is a key factor, Riverside remains a regular fly fishing base for members of the ownership families.

Several generations of river guides, and of family members, have been involved through the years, rich in McKenzie history. None of it likely would've happened had not one of the business principals been a globetrotting angler and one-time member of our fly-club. But let Lou S. Kennedy, his partner, tell the story:

"Before moving north, I was working as pier superintendent for Williams Diamond & Company and Neill Whisnant was our stevedoring manager. It was Neill who first introduced Donna and me to the McKenzie River.

"We first rented a cottage, now known as Wayfarer, situated where Martin Creek enters the McKenzie. In 1964 we bought Riverview Lodge from Daisy and Lou Brooks. That winter we had the heavy flood and there was eighteen inches of water on the lower floor. The front porch underpinning was completely undermined by the water and the front end of the lodge was about to fall into the river. Our guides at the time, Ennis Nestle and Merl McMullin, entered the lodge from the road by their drift boats and set the furniture out of reach of the water."

When an arsonist's fire leveled the original lodge in 1972, a new structure was operative the following year with Keith and Loretta Steele running it to serve the clients of Brady-Hamilton Stevedoring Co. as well as owner family friends. The Kennedys acquired Whisnant's share and when the company was sold, the Steeles took other employment. The lodge still is used March until November by family and friends and still generating memories both inside and out on the river. Kennedy:

"We once reeled in a rabbit, which had been chased into the river by a mink and was about to drown, and deposited it safely on the opposite shore. Weren't so lucky with a young otter, struggling to get out of a whirlpool! Ennis, my guide, had me net the creature, which then came out fighting, and in the process of recapturing him one of us got bitten. Eventually we placed him ashore, to his — and our — pleasure!"

Riverside's utilization of McKenzie river men reads like the roster of the guides association. In addition to Nestle and McMullin, there were the old timers — Rube Montgomery, Earl Jeans, John West, Ted Bryant, Frank Brown, Wayne Price, and Butch Taylor. Then, the day's fee was only $25. More recently, Riverside engaged Greg White, Dan Stucky, Gary Williams, Gene Highfill, Jim Goodpasture, Don Dill ... "and others as the occasions arose."

Don Wouda is now Riverside's No. 1 guide. And each season his most enthusiastic angling client is Donna Kennedy. Wouda:

"She has been a McKenzie regular for the past fifty years, and still fishes more than a dozen times a season, rain or shine!"

Wouda also has what has become a traditional date each season with the son of the late Neill Whisnant, Bruce:

"Once I had learned the basics from Ennis, Dad fine-tuned my fly fishing skills and our great days on the McKenzie continued until some time before his death in mid-July of 1993. The very next season I initiated the annual "Neill Whisnant Memorial Day." Each June, Don Wouda and I fish a favorite stretch of Dad's, above McKenzie Bridge.

"Immediately upon catching and releasing our first oversize redside, we pull ashore, drink a chilled bottle of Chardonnay and reminisce about Dad, an accomplished and ever-enthusiastic fly fisherman. Providently, we have taken at least one qualifying fish each "Memorial Day"."

Bruce's McKenzie companion through their high school and University of Oregon years was the Kennedy's son, Jim. Bruce:

"We fished nearly every feeder stream of the McKenzie system that held fish of any size. And we utilized the old log cabin Wayfarer for "extended" social functions with our university friends. One winter we had so much snow we couldn't make it down the driveway.

"The architectural design of the new Riverside Lodge, which Lou and Dad drafted on a napkin stained with a little gin, well fits the lay of the land and the interior's traffic pattern is of a fishing lodge superior! Many of the business customers were from Japan who also enjoyed rounds of golf at Tokatee to complement their McKenzie fishing experiences."

McKenzie River Highway

Photograph courtesy Lane County Pioneer Museum

An Appreciation

Essay appearing in the July, 1987, issue of Life Magazine

By Barry Lopez

For the past 18 years I've lived on the McKenzie River in western Oregon. I think I could tell the voice of this river against the voices of other rivers, but I would not like to be tested.

I traveled into the Canadian Arctic, to Japan and southern Africa during those years. I always come home to this river. By its seethe and purl, the sight of mergansers landing on it, the tug of it against my thighs, I recover some sense of who I am.

From its supple shoulders, sadly, I can see a stark counterpane of barbered forest. I know herbicides have leached into it and that dams have changed its personality. I used to think such an aggressive employment of the land—the feeder creeks choked with logging debris, the salmon beds lost—needed urgent attending to. It does. But there's a broader issue here.

Nancy Evelyn photo

Gradually, over several millenia, we've traded in a fraternal or companionable relationship with the land for an economic one—the land as thing. When I return after a long journey, I do not find myself wishing only to preserve this river, which consoles and edifies and pulls at me with its complexity—I want to preserve the ground of our relationship. It is founded, for my part, on regard for the mystery inherent in all life, including forms as obscure as this river. From this attitude of respect are derived my sense of home, of responsibility to community, and the admonition to lead and dignified and compassionate life.

If we do not retrieve and nurture, I think, some more gracious relationship with the land, we will find our sanctuaries, in the end, have become nothing more that commodities. They will not be the inviolate and healing places we yearn for, but landscapes related to no one.

Not in My Kitchen!

As usual, Victor Jules Bergeron pushed the envelope too far. He was hustled out of the kitchen of Riverview Lodge and, it is said, never again returned to that McKenzie facility with his cadre of fishermen followers.

The event might've been quickly forgotten—except that Mr. Bergeron was more universally known as Trader Vic! The incident might not have even happened, except that Keith Steele, who then was leasing Riverview with his wife, Loretta, had a real short fuse.

Those directly involved are gone now, though Mrs. Steele in recent years still remembered Trader Vic as "... a pain in the you know what!" according to Dave Helfrich. It is conceded along the river that Husband Keith was a master drift boat builder equally known for a very quick temper.

A lesser iron-willed couple than the Steeles might've been more deferential to the man TIME magazine described as "...irascible, ingenious restaurateur who, starting in 1934, parlayed a tiny beer tavern in Oakland, CA, into a San Francisco-based food and drink corporation grossing $50 million a year and featuring an international chain of 21 restaurants..."

But the Steeles, being independent river folk, weren't impressed. So when Vic invaded Loretta's domain, where she herself was an excellent cook, "... she let him know that he could run his kitchens the way he wanted, but she was running hers her way!" according to Helfrich. When Vic persisted, the inevitable happened. Lew Kennedy:

"Vic for the past couple of years had been staying at the lodge with his entourage of guests. But his hurried exit from the (Steele's) kitchen prompted him to immediately cancel his reservations and never return to Riverside Lodge."

Excerpt from 2/2/98 letter to Ed Francis from Lou Kennedy

"I received your letter dated January 28, 1998, concerning the Trader Vic incident when he invaded the Steele's kitchen at Riverview Lodge on the McKenzie River, and proceeded to tell Loretta, Keith's wife, who is an excellent cook, how he wanted his dinner prepared.

"Now, as you may or may not know, Keith Steele had a "short fuse" and was never known for his diplomacy. He took it upon himself to explain in no uncertain terms, he never invaded one of Vic's kitchens, telling them how to prepare his meal! And, therefore, he didn't appreciate Vic's intrusion into his kitchen.... bothering his wife ... making her nervous ... and (by) telling her how to cook.

"Although I was not present during this encounter, I was told Keith literally kicked him out of the kitchen!"

> Five o'clock and the late Oregon light had turned the river to ribbon. Not the deadly dull of polyester, but the watery luster of silk. Seasons imitate nothing. Vine maple leaves hovered in the air between evergreens. Vermilion on emerald. Sockeye salmon colors. Down below wild rainbows and steelhead would have magenta spawning stripes blasting down their flanks. October on the McKenzie.
>
> From "The Master of Redside Riffle" by Jessica Maxwell.

Chapter 6

McKenzie Fish

Guide Greg White about to release a 20-inch native redsides.

McKENZIE STEELHEAD

Early day steelheaders — unless they also prized rainbow, cutthroat and bull trout and Chinook salmon — never gave the McKenzie River a second look. That's because there was no wild native race and no successful hatchery plants of steelhead in the river until 1972!

And that explains why those early chasers of ironheads passed up the otherwise bountiful McKenzie. This club's first president, J.W. "Mike" Kennedy didn't even pause in his trips between Oregon's lower Rogue and Washington's Kalama. And Mike was known as "Mr. Steelhead" throughout the entire Pacific Northwest!

Small wonder the prominent steelheaders of that day had nothing to say of the McKenzie. Claude M. Kreider in his "Steelhead" (G.P. Putnam, NY, 1948) omits the McKenzie from his list of 18 Oregon rivers.

The focus of equally prominent Clark C. Van Fleet, in his "Steelhead to a Fly" (Atlantic Monthly Press, Boston, 1951) was on the nearby North Umpqua.

It wasn't until Trey Combs brought out his "Steelhead Flyfishing,' (Lyons & Burford Pubs., NY, 1991) that the McKenzie began to get national attention. Combs considered Ron Van Iderstine of Springfield " ... the best steelhead and salmon guide that I have ever known."

In part, Combs explained, because his Ron Van Iderstine's "RVI" fly gave Combs " ... evenings where steelhead took this fly on every cast. I rose ten fish and landed seven on my best evening with the light orange version."

Another local expert Combs pays homage to is Mike Brooks of Veneta, OR, "... whose home waters are ... most notably the McKenzie downstream Leaburg Dam." After more than twenty years of close watch, Brooks claims fly patterns more important than " ... presentation or tackle or technique." Combs favored the General Practitioner fly, but often switched to the beautiful and difficult dressings of the McKenzie Sapphire Nos.1 and 2.

The McKenzie is a late-bloomer for steelhead for several reasons, according to Robert Hooton, natural fish production manager for the Oregon Department of Fish & Wildlife. Hooton:

"It would be accurate to state that the resident form of rainbow trout (*Oncorhynchus mykiss*) was present in the McKenzie many thousands of years prior to steelhead being introduced.

"Recent genetic analysis indicates these fish a quite unique and ancient form of rainbow trout, different from your typical coastal rainbow or eastside redband trout."

Hooton points out that the Willamette Basin's native steelhead are from a more recent — but still thousands of years ago — invasion of coastal *O. mykiss*, which, for whatever reason, did not advance upstream from the Calapooya subbasin.

"Another piece of the puzzle," Hooton adds, "is that a unique fish disease, *Ceratomyxa shasta* (sorry, there is no common name) also invaded up the Willamette to Corvallis, but apparently no higher in the basin. The ramifications of this soon will become apparent."

C. shasta was not universally fatal. Native Rogue stocks were resistant, Umpqua stocks were not; also both steelhead and rainbow stocks of coastal streams. Are McKenzie rainbow trout resistant? Perhaps. Native winter steelhead from the Santiam are resistant, for example, since they may never have been exposed to the disease.

Getting a steelhead run established in the McKenzie wasn't easy. Trask River fingerlings stocked from 1911 to 1913 did not survive. Possibly, Hooton speculates:

" ... because of exposure to *C. shasta* in the lower Willamette when they migrated out as smolts, or they didn't survive to smolt size because of competition with more numerous native rainbow juveniles."

Fish in the first ever steelhead stocking in the McKenzie, in 1968 and 1969, also did not survive. They were Siletz summer steelhead smolts and also succumbed to *C. shasta*. A McKenzie steelhead fishery was in doubt until 1972. Hooton:

"The first successful plants came from releases of 110,000 smolts of Skamania (Washougal River) stock summer steelhead—with a few Klickitat River thrown in."

And so began the McKenzie's summer run. But what about winter run fish? From his records, Hooton determines there was no really serious attempt to stock winter steelhead. How then? Hooton explains:

"They started showing up as strays in the lower McKenzie in the mid-Fifties after the Fish Commission planted North Santiam stock, from Marion Forks Hatchery, in Fall Creek and the Middle Fork Willamette.

"Anglers would catch a few after the trout season opened in late April. The Santiam winter stock is often late running, contingent upon passage conditions at Oregon City Falls. Less than two dozen winter stock passed Leaburg Dam annually in the late spring.

"Counts began at Leaburg in 1957, but it wasn't determined until 1975 that most fish now were summer steelhead."

As the summer steelhead runs grew, so did the fishermen's experiences—and stories—about them. Yarns of unusual Redside angling generally got top billing in any view of the McKenzie, but steelhead themselves account for some really heavyweight stories.

The late icon guide Merl "Mac" McMullin had his share. Mac:

"A young doctor, Bob Bain of Salem, OR, was trying dry flies up towards Blue River. Fishing was slow and many flies tried, the last a Renegade or Buzz Hackle, Size 14. First thing we knew, out came a big steelhead and took that little fly!"

The doctor had been dry-flying upstream, a McMullin specialty, and the fish jumped three times before leaping into the boat. McMullin:

"I thought, this is one for my lifetime! I'll never see this happen again! But maybe six years later, right above our house, a fellow from California had a steelhead jump in a circle around our boat until it came in over the oarlock and landed at my feet ... a nine-pounder! After the excitement died down a little, the fellow spoke up and said—

'Well, I didn't get much play out of that one!'"

McMullin's final steelhead recall, pre-1990, was anticlimactic. His guiding day was ending as evening shadows began to fall. A lady from New York was playing a big fish. Her husband tried to get a picture as it was being brought to net.

"But in the excitement," Mac recalled, "he managed to lose overboard the last flashbulb for his camera!"

One of the grand lady anglers of the upper McKenzie, has visited her riverside cabin each season from her San Rafael, CA, home base for nearly a half century. (A more complete story of Dixie Monkhouse appears elsewhere.) Here she describes her steelhead highlight memories:

"For twenty years I had as my guide Ennis Nestle, and we had wonderful fishing together until his retirement in the early 1980s. So when I got this steelhead on, with Ennis, he took me over Martin Rapids! I'll never forget going over the rapids with that steelhead! A memorable day!"

Guide Nestle was involved in yet another of that family's steelhead fortunes. Dixie:

"My niece and her husband came here on their first anniversary and went out fishing with Ennis. They got five steelhead! They didn't know what they were doing! Couldn't believe it! Yes, beginner's luck! Absolutely! And Ennis had never before caught that many in one day!"

McKENZIE BULL TROUT

FACT & FANCY

Next to the storied Metolius, the upper McKenzie River is the Oregon stronghold of the bull trout. This from, among others, Jim Berl, a veteran McKenzie guide whose specialties include introducing some clients to that poorly understood and often badly treated game fish.

For most of the past century, and even before, *Salvelinus confluentus* aka the Dolly Varden, has struggled to survive where ever man hadn't yet lethally heated or polluted the Dolly's cold, clear domain. In declaring the bull trout as a threatened species, a U.S. Fish & Wildlife spokesman in 1999 commented: " ... we're saying that we've got some sick watersheds out there."

And, even sick humor of long standing. The Portland OREGONIAN in its October 14, 1915, issue reported:

"'Uncle George' Frissell is the most successful catcher of Dollies ... he keeps a long, stout cane pole with a big spoon hook on it in constant readiness on (the McKenzie River) bank and there, every few days, he 'snakes out a big one.'

"'He does it in self-defense, he says, for in the winter when the river is high' ... the Dollies come into the garden and eat the cabbages, and roost on the limbs of the apple tree, by golly, and break 'em with their weight.' "

Dollies do, indeed, have all but insatiable appetites, allowing the survivors to sometimes reach astonishing heft. Of McKenzie bull trout, high up the river's main stem or in the South Fork canyon, below Cougar Dam, Doc Crawford in his informative "Driftboater's Guide:"

" ...the last big Dolly caught on the McKenzie, a twenty-plus pounder, was caught out of the Blue Hole in the late Fifties."

Yet on July 3, 1977, in the Eugene REGISTER-GUARD, staffer Pete Cornaccia reported, in a tongue-in-cheek mode, having observed a South Fork bull trout as follows:

"Lord, he — or she — was big! Not quite forty pounds or three arms long, in my estimation, but big enough to have Don Latham's 12 1/2-pounder for breakfast and still feel hungry."

From the early third of the last century until as late as 1980, public, and even professional, ignorance of the bull trout was commonplace. And today, many still aren't aware the bull trout is different from its look-alike cousin. Anglers use the names interchangeably.

At one time, the Dolly was thought to be the only raider of salmon spawning beds, and was killed for the bounty on its tail. Those surviving had to cope in streams warmed alarmingly when loggers clear-cut the bankside Douglas fir, cedar and hemlock that once afforded shade. Land-clearing developments increased the pollution of runoff waters. Introduction of aggressive, non-native trout favored by anglers also spurred the bull trout's decline.

The news is better today in the McKenzie Valley watershed. Especially, according to Guide Berl, the bull trout enhancement in Sweetwater, Anderson, and Ollallie creeks systems.

Berl only keeps track of the length of bull trout released from his boat because weighing them might jeopardize the fish's chances of survival. So far, a 32-inch monster tops his list and his memories of them.

He describes his taking fly — Purple Flashbugger — as a leach representation on 3X long Size 4 or 6 hooks with brass bead head.

Berl's love and respect for the things that fly fishing stand for comes naturally. His maternal grandmother, Rosalie Hellman, was an avid fly fisher of the McKenzie, and Jim started out on the river with bicycle and fishing rod when just twelve years old. He developed his river running skills on the Grande Ronde and John Day's North Fork before returning to the McKenzie to guide in 1984.

LANE COUNTY BOUNTY

During the last three years there has (sic) been more large fish caught-- from two to 5 1/2 pounds— than I ever knew of and I have been fishing the streams of Lane County for twenty-five years. Another reason is that the stopping of the big log drives has been a benefit to spawning fish of the Willamette and the McKenzie rivers— the two best rainbow streams in the State of Oregon.

"The South Fork of the McKenzie is noted for the Dolly Varden trout. It is a wonderful stream. The McKenzie has been fished more than any other stream in the county on account of the good country road that parallels it. Many of the rainbow caught weigh from 3 1/2 to 4 1/2 pounds and some as high as 5 1/2 pounds."

Game Warden E.C. Hills under title, "Good Fishing in Lane County— the Reason," published in the 1916 OREGON SPORTSMAN by William L. Finley when he headed the old Oregon Game Commission.

"Today we don't fully grasp the impact of early logging in Oregon which concentrated along the rivers for ease of access and for the great log drives employed to get the timber down to the mills. The rivers were the log roads! There were so-called navigation companies employed by the timbermen just to clear the streams of obstacles and this included channeling and blasting and removing natural instream cover logs that created the hydraulics for pool and riffle."

—*Tom McAllister, McKenzie Creel Historian*

CHAPTER 7

FLY TIERS

HERM ELLINGSEN/BILL HUNT

Bill Hunt, early day sporting goods store operator on outskirts of Eugene, had lower McKenzie waters pretty much figured out. A dresser of popular early McKenzie patterns, Hunt was invited to contribute to this journal but resisted many contact efforts. It was his custom to keep his hard-won "secrets" to himself. But with Herman Ellingsen, a McKenzie fishing partner, 1954-1970, it was a different story.

Ellingsen, son of a Coos County sheriff and grandson of a trading schooner captain, Ole Peter Ellingsen, had settled in Eugene, headquarters of Ellingsen & Warner Construction Company.

Ellingsen was born (1913) and raised in Coquille, where his dad got him fly-fishing on the Rogue before his 'teens. But, as Ellingsen recently admitted: "I fished and fished but, y'know, at twelve you're really not much of a fisherman."

He was a fairly accomplished angler upon meeting Bill Hunt and recalls that Bill:

"Was a hard man to get to know. Kinda grumpy. Didn't give away his secrets very fast. But Bill was tops among fishermen I ever fished with. And his language often was pretty colorful.

"He thought like a fish. Had the most fantastic eyesight! He could tell, with one roll of a steelhead, whether it was a buck or a doe!"

Hunt and Ellingsen paired off well together for sixteen years. Some winters they were fishing on the Siuslaw and other coastal rivers. Yet McKenzie trips were the glue of their friendship. Hunt had quit Mckenzie guiding mostly because his "dudes" too often were inept fly-fishermen. Hunt and Ellingsen were a deadly pair:

"This is going to sound like a lie, but I don't think I ever fished the upper McKenzie with Bill that we didn't catch somewhere's around a hundred fish—or more!" Ellingsen re-called. "They were the old McKenzie redsides!"

The deadly duo had occasion to badger one another, as Ellingsen remembers:

"We were way upriver, among big rocks and boulders, where it's all pocket water fishing. Bill fished with no luck until allowing, 'It's your turn, drop the oars and I'll take 'em!' "

Ellingsen chose an area where he could dangle his two-fly setup alternately in a series of potholes. Finally. before Ellingsen began to pick up fish, Hunt exploded:

"What-the-hell you doin' ... tryin' to scare every fish out of the river!?!"

Ellingsen knew that Hunt had a Pennsylvania background where most trout were wary German browns. Even so, his response was:

"You row ... I'll fish!"

At another hot spot on another McKenzie trip, Ellingsen was casting and Hunt was rowing. After Ellingsen had picked up his fourth double on eight casts, Hunt exclaimed:

"My turn!"

Hunt's first cast hooked one fish. As he was bringing it in, Ellingsen observed if Hunt couldn't fish any better than that he should get back on the oars. Instead, Hunt gave a name to his incoming fish, gave it slack line and urged:

"Go get 'em George!"

According to Ellingsen, "George swam out a ways and Bill's fly picked up a second fish. That one got off, but was replaced by another redside. Four fish hooked on one cast! At that point Hunt said:

"Old George is getting tired, let's turn George loose!"

Though neither of them knew it at the time, Ellingsen's mastery of McKenzie fishing would lead to his comeuppance when he moved to the banks of the Rogue River. Ellingsen:

"Until I finally learned that Rogue half-pounders will hook themselves, I popped off a lot of nice fish! On McKenzie trout, you had to set the hook!"

The miles between the Rogue and the McKenzie put an end to their fishing companionship, but not their friendship. Ellingsen:

"Haven't seen Bill now for some time, but usually on my trips to Portland, I stop by his little fly tying place on Hayden Bridge Road. We always chat up storm."

"THE WORLD'S BEST!"

Decades before fly tying evolved into today's art form, durability and floatability of the dressing was most admired by active anglers. Then, customers of Smith and Stella Ely counted themselves most fortunate on that score. Their bugs were built to be buoyant! The couple's shop was based in Blue River, but their popularity extended well beyond the McKenzie Valley.

Smith Ely was an early and expert wader of the McKenzie and a rarity astream. He carried a kit for streamside tying. So many sought his counsel that he encouraged Stella to give fly tying priority over the ceramics and hand painted china she was creating and selling in their little shop. Most of their shop's flies were tied by Stella, once her deft fingers hugely out produced those of her husband, who often had "other fish to fry."

Foremost among Ely fly fans was the late Donald H. Bates, Sr., an honorary member of this club. By age ten, Bates had begun trouting, and before his second decade closed used only artificial flies. His maritime insurance enterprise helped take him to the earth's four corners. He fly-fished in various U. S. states, Canada, England, Scotland, Central and South America, New Zealand and Japan. Of Stella's dry flies, he wrote:

"... after much experience with fly makers, I must acknowledge her as the master of them all—The World's Best!"

Don Bates was one to put his money where his mouth was. As Stella was nearing retirement to Florence, OR, shortly after death of her husband, Bates commissioned her to do one hundred samples of her upright winged dry flies for framing. He also acquired her tying tools and supplies for archival stewardship by the Flyfishers Club of Oregon. And, he caused to be published a limited private edition, "Stella Ely, a Tribute."

In it, Clark C. Van Fleet, celebrated Pacific Coast angler, penned:

"Without a doubt, Stella Ely's flies were among the best for the McKenzie, Deschutes and many other rivers in the northwest. They were well and strongly made, true to pattern ... and perfect for the deep runs, long glides and underwater gravel banks that the McKenzie redsides love so well ... and I counted myself most fortunate to be one of her customers."

Another staunch Ely admirer was the late William J. Wood of Portland. Responding to Bates' furnishing two special Ely patterns, Wood in 1965 wrote:

"My untold appreciation to you for ... parting with those two original Ely flies. I was almost overcome—I couldn't believe it! They will never touch the water. I will use them to get copies made ... whenever I can find a possible reliable source."

Memories of the Stella Ely era—she died in early 1961, four years after her husband's death—remain vivid today for a host of contemporary McKenzie anglers.

"They tied good flies," Guide Dave Helfrich recalls. "Their gray drake was one of the best!"

After more than half-century of living on and fishing the McKenzie, Doug Walwyn remembers that Smith Ely, upon catching a large fish, would make a cardboard outline of it. Walwyn:

"He had them hanging all over the shop!"

Many McKenzie guides bought Ely flies for their clients, until learning to tie their own. Prominent among them was the late Merl "Mac" McMullin. His daughter, Joan DeCamara:

"I remember it well as a little girl—the three McMullin children rode with Mom and Dad in the vehicle towing the boat upriver to put in for the morning's drift. We'd make a stop every morning at Ely's for flies. I believe Dad used both natural bugs and Ely flies as samples to eventually make his own flies. I'm sure many McKenzie River guides did."

What Stella Ely fans couldn't have known was that, beyond her natural talent, she had formal schooling in two disciplines helpful in dressing flies. In the Midwest she studied art and optometry to a degree she became an inspector of lenses. Despite the awesome workload at her tying vise, Stella Ely filled many fly orders—including one for a thousand dozen from Meier & Frank's store in Portland—she somehow she found time for other interests. Using her kitchen range as an electric kiln, she turned out various ceramics and hand painted china. And, to create oil paintings and watercolors worthy of exhibition at Oregon's centennial fair.

Husband Smith had a varied and wide-ranging career, as civil engineer and realtor, before settling on the McKenzie, possibly because, it was said. he had an interest in the Blue Bird mine there.

The full story of Stella and Smith Ely and their super flies will never be told. She had tried teaching her techniques to others, but with poor results.

She was engaged in writing and illustrating a book on her special techniques when overtaken by death. That book surely would've occupied a prominent place in western fly dressing literature. All that remains now, beyond her fly dressing equipment, however, are dimming memories and scattered samples of her artistry in collections of aging admirers.

JOHN DOSE

The gypsy-like lifestyle of John Dose, sometime McKenzie angler and fly dresser, precluded much being known or remembered about him. With rare exception, he left a pretty cold trail.

In one such instance, 19 July 1941, he wrote a two-page letter in lovely Spencerian longhand to the late Lee Richardson, distinguished outdoor author and active supporter of our club. Then headquartered in an old bus, parked on the west end of Vida, Dose explained his move from the Rogue to the McKenzie thusly:

"The reason I quit the lower river was that you had to carry your own rock to fish off of. And generally, someone would push you off and take your place. I do not care to be shoved around when I am trying to fish!"

When Guide Prince Helfrich went to Dose's place for flies for clients, he often was accompanied by his eldest son, Dave, who remembers:

"What impressed me as a kid was the smell! Giving him the benefit of the doubt, maybe it was the combination curing hides and feathers he used in fly tying. Then again, it may have been because of limited bathing facilities on his bus."

Helfrich remembers Dose did tie a good fly:

"His Beetle Bug was a real fish catcher!"

Yet Dose is better remembered for his Dose Fly.

Chapter 8

Epilogue

Photo courtesy of Eugene Register-Guard

McKenzie/FFF icons (from left): Bill Nelson, Stan Walters, Skip Hosfield.

Where the Federation of Flyfishers Was Born

Temperate clime and abundant waters made possible—beyond great fishing opportunities—an extraordinarily fertile atmosphere generating noteworthy related activities in the country called McKenzie. No doubt most remarkable were mid-Sixties events giving birth to the Federation of Fly fishermen.

Energized by his innovative leadership role in the Evergreen Fly Club in Everett, WA, Bill Nelson, then a self-anointed "tire peddler," rolled into Eugene with a unique vision and boundless enthusiasm with which to execute it. But first, he had to harness existing but latent energy. He recalls his solution:

"I put an ad in the paper and it was answered by a few people who still are members of what became the McKenzie Fly fishers. We had a meeting in my house and then and there decided to do a fly club!"

One of those few early birds, J. D. "Skip" Hosfield, still remembers:

"At our second-ever meeting, President Nelson outlined an ambitious first-year program—including hosting a conclave to promote a national fly fishing organization! About half the members objected—and quit. The remaining believers began organizing while Bill went on the road lining up support of regional clubs and individuals. He secured Lee Wulff's commitment, giving the concept national credibility. Somehow, over the next twelve months, it all came together and the FFF was aborning!"

While Nelson was the elan vital, other "young tigers" including Hosfield were Stanley Walters, who became first Conclave chairman, and Riley Woodford, tireless host club vice president. All, except Woodford, who died young, remain fly fishing forces in Eugene—and beyond.

A decade after the FFF launching, another partial vacuum in Eugene received attention. Bob Guard, whose boyhood fishing of the Willamette's Coast Fork evolved into serious fly-fishing, couldn't find a No. 5 line in town. So, he started the Caddis Fly Angling Shop near Eugene's Amtrak Station. Fly fishing opportunities were close at hand. Guard:

"Armitage Park, two miles above the McKenzie's confluence with the Willamette, is in the city limits. In season, lunch time often finds sport jacketed or suited anglers with fly rods as common as yellow daffodils along the two hundred yards of bike path paralleling the McKenzie River, just below the park's boat put-in."

Guard and his late wife, Kathy, concentrated on offering the widest variety of equipment and tackle, most current fishing advisories and proven professional guiding service. Bob Houghton, now a respected Oregon outfitter, was a salesman and fly tier in early Caddis Fly days. When Guard sold out in 1995 it was to Chris Daughters, whom Guard had hired to work for him when he was only twelve years old. Daughters has carried on Caddis Fly traditions—and more.

THE CLASSIC CAST

Without doubt the locale of this prohibition era was the Willamette valley, out of Salem. And it's likely the specific was a wadeable stretch of what was first known "the Mckenzie fork of the Willamette Valley." We proceed: the young lad now knee deep in a McKenzie riffle, had convinced an elderly friend of the family to provide instruction on the art of fly-fishing. He was old country, with old country ways, and a bit of an accent. However, in place of the traditional English five pound note, he substituted his small flask of moonshine under his pupil's casting arm. It would be a constant reminder of the importance of keeping that arm tight against his side: "now, don't cha break me heart, lad! You knows how I loves my whiskey!"

BLUE RIVER—When the world's trout fishermen talk of Oregon, they think about its king of rivers, the Rogue, and its queen, the Deschutes.

But the aristocracy is incomplete with outside glimpses at Prince Umpqua and the princess of all rivers—the delicate, delectable and deceptive McKenzie.

Flushed from a lake famed for its clarity and embraced for nearly its entire route by an emerald canopy, the McKenzie passionately tumbles and muscles its way out of the Cascade Mountains over stones, pebbles and boulders easily visible in even the deepest blue-green holes.

Her kisses on the skin of a boat or raft are alternately tender and temperamental. Soft, billowing currents often erupt into white-water fury as the river bends and dives, scrambling to catch up with its wayward downhill path.

The watery highway leaves indelible memories.

—Bill Monroe

THE OREGONIAN, 9 July 1982

McKENZIE RIVER TRUST

GIVING BACK TO THE RIVER

The bounty of the McKenzie River Valley, and the need to see that bounty protected for future generations, is the reason the McKenzie River Trust was chartered as a non-profit corporation in 1989.

Nearly a century ago, the Drury family settled in the upper valley along the West Fork of Horse Creek, which was highly regarded by anglers. Side tributaries of Horse Creek, Taylor and Drury Creeks, were and remain fry and fingerling rearing quarters. At one time, the late Bob Drury fed cottage cheese to a dozen or so big bull trout temporarily held in a shallow, shaded, spring-fed pond on his place.

Owners of the 25-acre parcel, Drury and wife, Cam, and Jim and Mary Jane Drury, knew they were stewards of something special. The high quality riparian assets included hillside wooded land which they had only partially logged in 1993 and was reestablishing well with remaining trees, browse brush and forb. As result, elk and deer established wintering grounds during periods of deep snow or intense cold spells.

MRT was only six years old when the Drury Donation began to take shape. For $l, Jim and Mary Jane gave first purchase option for the half-interest. Later, in view of high medical needs and costs, the half of Bob and Cam's was purchased for $30,000. Final settlement took place in the fall of 1995. That phase was a win-win situation for the participating MRT and the Rocky Mountain Elk Foundation.

And eventually, when MRT resold the property at a later and higher appraised value to the U.S. Forest Service, once it had monies, the difference between the original cost and the amount paid by the USFS became seed money for yet other MRT projects!

More recently, MRT obtained a $500,000 grant from the Eugene Water & Electric Board, combined with a $500,000 challenge matching grant also from EWEB, for critical land acquisition along the McKenzie River corridor. The McKenzie Watershed Council is to determine riparian and water channel acquisition sites, particularly in the lower valley below Leaburg where development pressure is most intense.

More information about MRT is available from Craig McKern (email: cem9th@clipper.net) or visiting MRT's web page at www.mckenzieriver.org.